Mirror/Mirror

A Holistic Approach to Living Well

by
Denny Richard

b'leaf!

(growth requires shedding old beliefs)

Copyright © 2011 Denny Richard

www.dennyrichard.com

All rights reserved.

DEDICATION

For Mom

For all that you never had, you gave to me unconditionally.

CONTENTS

	Acknowledgments	i
	Preface	ii
	The Fool	1
	Stripped	3
1	Mirror/Mirror	4
2	Being Intentional With Words	7
3	Anyone Can Write	10
4	Choose Your Mood	14
5	10 Things that can Improve Your Happiness	17
6	What Does Yoga Mean?	21
7	Yoga and Repressed Emotions	24
8	Fall in Love Again	27
9	Loving You is Easy, Because I Love Me	30
10	Body	33
11	Working Out	36
12	Yoga for Athletes	39
13	Spring Cleaning	43
14	Balance	47
15	Change	50

16	Nutrition - It Isn't Easy Being Green	52
17	Ayurveda 101 - The Brief Intro	55
18	The Food We Eat	59
19	The In and the Out	64
20	Conflict	67
21	An Observer's Guide to a Healthy Relationship	71
22	Do You Mind?	73
23	Oh My Pernicious Mind	77
24	The Kleshas	85
25	The Veil of "Miss Perception"	89
26	Recovery	92
27	The Fog	95
28	A Walk Into Silence	96

29	Journal Entries:
	    on Love
	    on Sleep
	    on Like/Dislike
	    on Relationships
	    on Parenting
		99

30	My Last Breath	105
	Resources	111
	About the Author	113

ACKNOWLEDGMENTS

Many people and events have guided the creation of this book. To whittle the experience down to one mere existence would not be a truth. My students, peers, and clients are my greatest teachers and I am honored to know you. The guidance and instruction from all of my teachers, especially the ones from the Seven Centers Yoga Arts in Sedona, AZ have been life changing. To my book reviewer, Paul Rivenberg, I really appreciate you diving in and guiding me. Tammy and Michael, thank you for your love and support, you guys shine light on my darkest hours.

This book would not be possible without the countless backers who donated their time, energy and funding to produce the book. Thank you to both Jonathan P. Quinn and Thomas Patrick Baer for your generous support. To all of you who contributed to the Funding Project, I am truly grateful.

As you noticed, on the back cover of the book 10% of all proceeds from the sales of this book are donated to HIV/AIDS Foundations to bring those living with HIV/AIDS support and to help find a cure. HIV/AIDS affects everyone. If you know of an organization that could use some support, please let me know.

Cover
The photos on the cover are images I shot in Arizona, Oregon, Yosemite Park and my hometown of Gardner, MA. The layout was inspired by Dann Dykas.

PREFACE

Mirror/Mirror is a collection of articles and journal entries written from 2006-2011 while I was in Phoenix, AZ. They are a culmination of teachings as well as lessons I have learned. Read straight through the book, or pick random chapters. My hopes for you, the reader, is that you gain insight on ways to live life fuller and happier. You have the most amazing potential inside of you, and the only one that gets in the way of that potential is you.

Belief. I mention several times in this book to not believe what is written in these pages. What is written here is my truth based on my experiences alone. I was guided by many teachers, tools and texts to come to my viewpoint and this is what I am sharing with you. I ask that you not blindly believe in the words, but let them be used as inspiration to your own self-discovery. If you use them as a mode to discover, you will find that the words here become your truth through experience. Then it becomes something to believe in.

Journal Entry: "You know what we judge ourselves for?? Not having it all figured out, but that's just insane, because there is nothing to figure out, it already is. The only thing that could be "more perfect" than this moment, would be if my mind could get out of the way for me to see it as it is! It always works, it always has, it always will. Just be."

THE FOOL

Only a fool wants to know his future. For as soon as he hears the prophecy he will spend the rest of eternity in anticipation of what is bound to be his biggest disappointment. The power of life lives solely in the present moment.

Denny Richard

STRIPPED

Here I stand,
watching my own reflection.
I am my own worst critic,
but not today.
I make a decision.
I will not pass judgment on my own self.
Today, I breathe.
I begin to undress,
focusing solely on my breath.
Each layer of clothing that comes off
is like a layer of misperception of my self.
I stand before my self,
naked,
stripped,
unprotected,
yet I am whole,
grounded,
alive.
I am meant to be as I am,
not as I wish I were.
I take another breath,
I allow myself to reflect on this stranger before me.
I begin to recognize him.
I understand who he is.
I feel love for him.
He is me and I him.
We are one.
I am whole.

(2006)

1. MIRROR/MIRROR

I often say that life is a mirror. That which you see out there is just a reflection of the creative Universe of the YOU within. They match. The interesting part is we are all co-creating. When we take ownership of our life, emotions, thoughts, understandings, habits, patterns, we become the creator of our life and can witness the process of creation happening. You are the micro of the macro. You are that which you have come from and will return to. You are the journey. You are full of love, compassion, truth, and understanding. These things are not separate from you, but perhaps you've just forgotten to be them. They are there for you, inside, a part of you, ready and waiting for you to scoop them up and embrace every part of them with your ever expanding existence.

You are the mirror that you see reflected back at you in everything you are surrounded by. It is all a part of you, cleverly disguised as something else. Have compassion for the things that make you want to react negatively. Have love for the things that make you want to feel pity. Shine the light of courage on the things that make you feel afraid. Find yourself a mirror. Get to know that person that looks back at you, not from the outside, but from deep within. Figure out what makes that person tick.

Be aware of the energy you are putting out to your external Universe. The more you talk about issues to other people the more it reinforces it to you. If you talk about negative qualities, things you do not like, then it reinforces it in YOU. You become that negative quality that you are talking about. Most of the "haters" spend all of their time talking about what it is they are hating. They have forgotten that they have the ability to live their own life peacefully and happily. The most insecure people judge others the most, because deep down inside their mind is continually passing judgement on their own existence.

Happy people spend their time talking about how they have found happiness. Perhaps it was a great book of inspiration, or a teacher, or a practice. Whatever it is, they want to share it with others. The more they share that happiness, the more it grows within them, and the happier they become. Once you've found your presence, your happiness, you will begin to teach others how to get there too. You can't not; it's what you must do.

Everything that has come into existence must also go out of existence. We are made of star dust. We are that which has been transformed from something that came before us. This too shall pass, and then we will become something else. Knowing this, it is easier to let go of the attachment to what we think something should be, because as soon as something 'becomes', it turns into something else. It is an existence of constant change.

What can we do with the time we have here in this life? We can certainly spend it in worry. We can spend it in hatred. We can spend it in loathing, distrust, revenge, anger, resentment, disappointment, betrayal or being the victim. But whose life is being SPENT that way. Don't you know that you can choose a different life? Don't you know that you can spend your life in happiness?

Pay attention, listen, not only to others but to the world. See the deeper meaning of things. Why are you hearing this song at that time? Why did that person call you in this moment? Notice. Investigate. Practice. Do not judge - you are only judging yourself. Mirror/Mirror - it reflects in both directions. Allow yourself to see the beauty in all things. If you are used to being negative, you must practice being happy. Practice! The only person who can save you from your own delusional mind is yourself. You are the one that must do the work, and you are worth it.

Spend the rest of today, and all day tomorrow, whispering sweet nothings to yourself. Tell yourself how special you are and how much you're worth the attention you are giving yourself. Remind yourself how much you love the person who looks back at you in the mirror.

2. BEING INTENTIONAL WITH WORDS

"The pen is mightier than the sword," says English author Edward Bulwer-Lytton, and we can't disagree with him at all. He is speaking of the power of words, or the power of the intention behind the words being spoken or written. How often do you pay attention to what you are saying, writing, thinking or posting on your social networking pages?

We know that saying things to others with a negative undertone is unhealthy, not only for them but for us. Yet, we find ourselves reacting and shooting off our mouths before we even realize what we've said. Gossip, slander, yelling hateful words, calling names are all part of what our quick-thinking minds do, and when these words come out of our mouths or are written about others, it creates harm. It creates feelings of separation, protection, neediness, helplessness and victimhood. Yet, we blame others for what we are saying ourselves. Where has our sense of ownership gone?

"Be the change you want to see in the world," we are told by Ghandi, yet how many of us believe that we have this ability? Practice saying kind things to others, learn to understand your perceived "enemy" so that you can get a better understanding of yourself. If your external life is your mirror, then you will see yourself in this other person.

The ones that push our buttons the hardest are showing us a part of our truth that we are fighting against. It's not that we have to become what we don't want to see or understand in another, but it gives us the opportunity to understand ourselves on a deeper level. Each deeper understanding we get of ourselves brings us to our truth, and ultimately our own internal well of happiness.

Spoken words have great power, especially if we are using them *against* someone or something. There is a karmic return to all of this bad mouthing that we have long since become ignorant to. Also, the words we choose to describe things in our lives have a much greater effect on our own well-being. Have you ever said, "I have to go to work?" Do you know what you are saying here? Can you recognize the damage in the words that are pushing your happiness away? It's choice - a word choice. Saying that you "HAVE" to go to work, is saying that you do not have free choice. Not only are you giving away your right to choose to go to work, but you're giving away your power. You have become a slave chaining yourself mentally and emotionally to your work.

The same emotional, energetic, thought relationship occurs when we are not feeling well. We tend to share the illness with anyone that will listen. We share it in the energetic, emotional and thought form of "I'm sick." For some of us, energetically sharing our "illness" gives us attention, and our mind is constantly craving attention. So, we find that being "sick" is a great way for us to be noticed. We also tend to OWN what it is that our bodies are going through. How can you ever be free of high blood pressure if you're constantly saying "I *have* high blood pressure." How about saying, "My body is currently afflicted with high blood pressure." Can you see a difference?

How much of your time are you spending with these types of words that have a negative impact on your life? I'm HIV Positive, I'm Type Two Diabetes, I'm Fat, I'm Not Worthy, I'm Angry, I'm ____ (fill in the blank). Are you really this? Are you really only this? Can you be labeled down to one mere existence of your ever expanding internal universe?

The pen, or thought, is much mightier than the sword. The obsessive thought of "I'm Fat," keeps us in the repetitive cycle of seeing ourselves as "fat," which then the Universe turns around and delivers right back to us. Practice saying, thinking and feeling a positive aspect of your life. My body is healing. I'm content, I'm peaceful, I'm happy, I'm fortunate. Do these words sound foreign to you? If so, practice being with them more often. Make them your friends. Get comfortable saying them to yourself. You're that important.

Begin to take ownership of your life by taking ownership of the power you have in creating your life. It all starts with a thought. Be intentional in your thinking and CHOOSE wisely the words you use to describe your life. Freedom comes from within, not from dropping bombs. Peace is yours if you're ready for it, and happiness is a choice if you remember you have that choice. *At any moment, I can choose to be happy.*

Jill Bolte Taylor, a brain scientist and author of "My Stroke of Insight," had a massive stroke at age 37. She had a substantial recovery period and a huge awakening to understanding her mind. As a scientist, she was able to witness the process of the stroke happening. What she realized during her beginning stages of recovery was that part of her brain did not recognize people. She had no recollection of her mother, but says she knew instantly that she was safe when the woman who was her mother walked into the hospital room. Her mother only brought in an energy of nurturing and care, not worry, anxiety, fright. We do not realize the energy we throw in other people's directions. We take all of our internal emotion and chaos and virtually vomit it onto anyone that is near us without knowing it's impact on the other person. As Ms. Taylor says, "Be responsible for the energy you are bringing to me."

Practice using words with a positive vibration. Notice if the words, I can't, don't, won't, come out of your mouth or run through your mind. Spend time finding the opposite of the negative. For example, if you find yourself saying "I can't figure this out", say instead, "The answers are on their way."

3. ANYONE CAN WRITE

Inspired by: Kathleen Adams, <u>The Way of the Journal</u> (A journal therapy workbook for healing).

We are surrounded by magical events. Life itself is a wondrous unfolding of the most beautifully pristine magic there is: Presence. We Humans have a wonderful way of exploring and sharing the various ways of life through our acute ability to communicate. We have an amazing gift of sharing our stories with others. Although, some of our communication skills could use a dusting off.

Writing is one of those mediums which allows us to share the gift of story, or to help ourselves dive deeper into our own path of self-discovery. Many of us would like to write, but we look at a blank page and instantly begin to panic. "How can I write?," "I can't do this," and of course, "I'm not a writer," tend to be some of the instant thoughts that arise.

Journal writing can begin to break the blocks of creativity, help us to unearth some of our more deep-rooted obstacles and allow us to organize our lives. Journal writing is a process that helps to get "what's IN" to a place "outside of us" so that we can take a closer look by being further away from it. For example, when you see your best friend going through misery you understand what is causing it, but because they're "in it," they can't see it. We experience those same things. When we write down random thought forms in various ways on pieces of paper bound and covered, we move chaotic, disorganized energy from within to a place that becomes usable and manageable.

When you go to your journal to write, do not expect what comes out to be "Perfect." From the *Journal's* perspective, it doesn't matter, and it certainly does not need to make sense, it just needs to happen. Also, do not feel you have to share your journal or that you need to explain why. If you are afraid someone will read your journal and attempt to use the words inside against you, then hide it. Keep it in your trunk. Hide it in the floor boards of your house. Make sure you feel safe. Give yourself a chance, trust that you have a voice, and hug your journal, after all, it will become a mirror for you.

I find that having a quiet place to write, maybe with a lit candle and a cup of tea, offers me a space of nurturing and comfort, allowing me to dive deeper into issues that might be just below my surface level of understanding. The Nitty Gritty kind of stuff. If I get to my journal and I just don't know where to begin, I try a handful of these warm ups: Stretching, meditating, doodling, deep breathing, or random thought writing. When it's time to begin, begin. Let your pen move across the page leaving traces of ink in form of word or otherwise. We all process information in a variety of ways. Some of us are visual, some are aural, some are hands on. If we create a ritual that is done EVERY time we sit down to write, sooner than later our subconscious will say... "Oh, Denny is sitting in his comfy chair with a cup of tea. It must be mind-dumping time." For some, a quick stroll around the neighborhood will work. For others, some yoga stretches or a warm bath. Play around until you find the "just right" thing for that moment, knowing this too will change.

You can begin by simply writing BREATHE at the top of the page. You may also want to write three words that describe your current feelings: Joy, Apprehension, Adventurous. There are a great number of writing techniques you can use to get yourself going. Taking a journal writing workshop or picking up a book about journal writing techniques will help you explore more avenues and possibilities.

Creating a containment (container) for your writing is a great way to say, "Hey, I don't need to figure it all out at once," especially if you find that you are getting overwhelmed with your process. A great container for writing is simply closing the journal and putting it away. Whatever is already written is contained. If you write something you don't want to reread without assistance, for instance a deeper rooted emotional complex that might be better worked with a counselor or guide, fold those pages in to alert you to proceed with caution when you pass through your journal again. Another type of containment is to write for a predetermined amount of time, say 5 minutes, start a timer, begin writing and when the timer goes off, stop writing. You can also contain your writing to "just two pages" and then stop.

Pacing yourself is just as important as containing what you are writing. Kay Adams, creator of **Journal to the Self** Writing Workshops and the Center for Journal Therapy, tells us to "Be a dolphin. Dive deep and surface. Go into the heart of the issue, then come sharply to the surface. Look around, grab some air, go back into the heart." Every time you come up for air, look at the word BREATHE and your three feeling words and take slow deep breaths. Then begin again, or if it is time, close the book and put it away.

You might want to **do a short meditation** before each writing session to help clear the mind. Sit in stillness and train your mind to be aware of the incoming and out going breath. You can also train the mind to search through the body to discover different sensations that you are feeling in the current moment. Sensations are things like pressure, itching, tickling, vibration, warmth, dryness, coolness, and moisture, and they are always happening in the present moment.

Date every entry. Doing this will allow you to put a sense of timeline to your journal, and it helps to discover patterns: seasonal, relationship, finance, career. It helps us to dissect our life-pie with more accuracy.

Keep what you write. Sometimes we write things down and have no idea why we are writing them, or what they mean. Then some later date in the future we open up one of your past journals and magically the words that we see are exactly what we need to read in that moment.

Write quickly. This keeps the ever judgmental ego mind OUT of the process and allows the deeper issues of what needs to be communicated to surface. Get to the bottom line of what you're writing faster without the internal editing process. The internal "critic" may be there while you're writing, but there is absolutely no need to listen to it.

Start writing and keep writing. Often when you first start to write, you'll put a couple of sentences down and the mind starts to judge what is there. In order to break through this, you have to keep writing. Otherwise, the journal closes with a triumphant mind saying, "You can't write." Here's a secret: ANYONE CAN WRITE. Grammar and spelling don't even count, and unless you're looking to get published, *"it won't mattar if every thing you right is incorrect or knot!"*

Protect your privacy. "**KEEP OUT - Please do not read any further than this page without my permission,**" is a simple way of reminding those that may come across your journal that some things are better left alone. Besides, the words you write inside of your book will mean nothing to anyone except you.

Write naturally without rules. There are plenty of guidelines and creative ways of getting the writing process going, but do not feel you have to conform to the rules. When it comes to journal writing, the rules of society should be ignored (and some of us are very fond of not conforming to societal rules).

Write it, you can.

Write a list of twenty things you are grateful for.
Write a list of twenty things you want to do (then pick five and do them).

4. CHOOSE YOUR MOOD

When it comes to mood, we often think that we're stuck with what we've got or what we're going through. For example, we wake up, stub our toe on the end of the bed and then step on a nice fresh hair ball happily regurgitated up by Fluffy in the wee small hours of the morning. One would think our mood would have to be sour to match the events. Imagine watching this as an episode on our favorite television comedy. We might instead find it quite funny. It's the personalization of the event that puts us into a "mood." We are quick to label things "happening to me," and when we do this, we become the victim of circumstance.

Our mood greatly depends upon our reaction to experiences and the thoughts we are associating with those experiences. The truth of it is, "life" is just happening out there. Nothing out there creates our mood. We create our mood. That mood is created by our reaction to the sensations occurring in our bodies. We don't like the feel of banging our toe on the end of the bed, and because we don't like it, we start to think negative thoughts about the experience. These negative thoughts begin to create a negative emotion, which we also do not like, so the negative thought story continues.

If you'd like to be free of dramatic "mood" and just be, which is typically a naturally happy place, then you'll need to become aware of the process of thought and emotion in terms of how it reacts to circumstance and situation. The thought process reacts in two directions - into the Past or into the Future. When you are in the present moment and aware of the fact that you're there, there is no thought. You are just experiencing what IS, as it happens. Past thoughts tend to relate to emotions based on regret, guilt, sadness (the should have, could have, would have). Whereas thoughts of the future tend to be towards fear, doubt, anxiety and worry (that which has not yet come to pass).

Step 1: Identify your current mood. Ask yourself, "How am I feeling right now?" Are you thinking about the past or future? Being aware of your current mood will help to move you to the present moment and out of the cycle of thought-emotion.

Step 2: Ask yourself, "who is responsible for this emotion?" If you are really determined and ready to feel different/better, you will know there is only one answer to this question, always. We often fall into the pattern of blaming anyone and everyone for how we feel. "He/She did this 'to me'." When the truth of it is, he/she did, and we reacted. You must own your own emotions, they belong to no one but you. You are the creator of your own emotional battlefield. When you first start to do this work, this can be one of the hardest things to overcome. But the only person in this whole Universe that is responsible for your happiness is YOU. So the absolute reverse must also be true. The only person in this whole Universe that is responsible for your unhappiness is YOU. (Isn't it great living in dualistic balance of opposites?)

Step 3: Take a big deep breathe and know that all can change (and does) in a single moment.

Step 4: Practice feeling better. Choose happiness. This is another thing that's hard to do in the beginning. If you're used to feeling bad or sad or depressed, or you spend your time worrying, then you'll actually have to practice feeling happy. When you are habitually feeling negative emotions, it's easy to fall back into that energy and space. That simply means, you are in the habit because you've been practicing it for so long. If you recognize your scenery, take a different turn.

When it comes to being happy or sad, remember you always have a choice, and it is always YOUR choice. We sometimes get caught up in the stories that brew in our overly active thoughts; then we fall victim to the story and become emotionally caught up. Also, be aware of who you're giving your attention to. Some people are REALLY good at spewing out negativity and misery, fully expecting you to jump in on their miserable parade, which is quite easy to do. We have to remember not to allow that to happen. Other people just do. If you find that your best friend Mary is a major source of negativity, and you start practicing happiness, the Universe will then turn around and create more space for you to live your life in happiness, which will mean less time with Mary. What do you choose?

Be conscious of the food, drink and "other" you're introducing to your body. These things also have a great effect on the thoughts that you think and the moods that you create. They do not call alcohol a depressant because it makes you think happy thoughts. Your nervous system is a reactionary existence. It reacts to what is going on in your external world, but also to what is going on with your body. When there is a substance flowing through the body, the mind will react to external situations differently based on the properties of the substance introduced and being experienced in the body.

Be aware, then take action from the mindset of awareness. Know that you have the ability to do this and put it to practice. Know that you are capable of being happy, and that you deserve happiness. You are the most amazing person in the Universe. If you do not believe this of yourself then say this to yourself in the mirror for 30 days:

YOU are the most amazing person in the Universe.
You ARE the most amazing person in the Universe.
You are THE most amazing person in the Universe.
You are the MOST amazing person in the Universe.
You are the most AMAZING person in the Universe.
You are the most amazing PERSON in the Universe.
You are the most amazing person IN the Universe.
You are the most amazing person in THE Universe.
You are the most amazing person in the UNIVERSE.

5. 10 THINGS THAT CAN IMPROVE YOUR HAPPINESS (<u>RIGHT NOW</u>)

When you are faced with the question, "How do I choose to be happy," use these items as a reference point to cultivate the happiness within and consider writing your own 10 guide points.

1. Start with your Breath. One of the quickest ways to get out of the chaotic thought patterns (which pull you away from the present moment and the place where happiness naturally dwells), is to become aware of your breathing. When you become aware of the breath coming in and out, you are training your mind to be present to the moment. Develop a slow and full bodied breath and watch your mood change to a calmer happier place. The reason is simple - Breath, is always present. It's always occurring in the present moment. It is always with you. It is your connector to life (which occurs in the present moment only). Breathing in is the first thing you do when you're born, and breathing out will be the last thing you do before you die. Yeah, it's important.

2. Take a Yoga Class. There is something about moving through a yoga class that help you feel better. One thing yoga does is helps you get in touch with your body. You know, the thing that you live in that helps your inside world and your outside world meet to experience each other. Yoga stretches the body, which makes the body less reactionary to external sensations (which makes the mind less reactionary to the body's experience of the external sensations). Yoga develops a deeper breath and understanding of the link between breath and life, and it cultivates awareness, all of which are essential parts of **being** happy. If you are new to yoga, look for a beginner's class, gentle/yin or restorative class.

3. Create a Gratitude List. A Gratitude List is a list of things you are grateful for right now. It reminds you that there are things in your life that constantly support you, and helps you to find your happiness within. If you're the type of person that constantly focuses on the negative aspects of something or someone (like most of us do), then creating a gratitude list about that person or something will help to remind you that you are choosing to see it that way. Write down "I am grateful for..." then create a list. If you look for the worst in someone, you'll find it. If you look for the best in someone, you'll find it.

4. Clean your systems. More often than not, your internal and external systems aren't very clean, and this not only creates havoc for your body, but it creates chaos for the mind. The sinuses can be cleaned with a neti pot, the tongue can be scraped, the teeth can be scrubbed and the body can be washed. When the systems are clear, the mind becomes clear and happiness flows freely. Take a long bath with candlelight and soft music. Seek the guidance of a Feng Shui advisor, or read a book or article on it (read Chapter 13 on Spring Cleaning). Clear your external spaces of unnecessary clutter (most of it is unnecessary). This will give the mind fewer opportunities to become distracted by it's ever judgmental opinions of "like" vs "dislike".

5. Sing or play music. When you look at anything under a microscope, you see the smallest part of that "thing" as vibration. Everything in the Universe is vibrating. The different frequencies of vibration create different "things" for you to experience. Music, or Sound is also a vibration. When you play or sing music, you are creating a vibration within to resonate at a different tune. Chanting, joining a chorus and singing songs that are light and fun will bring that happiness from the inside out. Playing music with a band will help create a melodic musical vibration, which also changes the internal systems to resonate at different frequencies. Time to dust off that instrument!

6. Meditate. If you are truly looking to get out of the chaotic mind patterns of past and future and want to train the mind to be present, then develop a meditation practice. Two things you can focus your attention on while you sit in silence and stillness are your Breath and also the Sensations that you experience in the body (things like pressure, itching, tickling, heat, coolness, moisture and dryness). All of these things are happening in the present moment (where life exists), and when you train your mind to be present to these things, you start to become happy. Your unhappy existence is due to the fact that your chaotic mind is constantly pulling you away into stories of past or future that have nothing to do with the present moment experience. (Hint: we do it to ourselves) (www.dhamma.org)

7. Eat Healthy. It can't be emphasized enough how what you put into your system has an effect on your overall health (body, mind and spirit). Your body is a micro Universe. A delicate eco-system of balance. When you are putting into that system things that are not good for balance, you get unbalance. Not only does the body feel this, but the thoughts and emotions become unbalanced and the mind becomes chaotic. This is not a happy place. Choose wisely what you put into your body and onto your body. (A general rule of thumb for what to put on your body - if you wouldn't put it in your mouth, don't lather it up on your skin. Stick to natural ingredients.)

8. Get a Massage. Massaging the body is a wonderful way to release toxins from the system. If you're uncertain on where to go, or what type to get, ask! If getting a massage from someone else isn't your thing, then start practicing Abhyanga. This is a daily ayurvedic self-massage using a balancing oil. Go ahead, look it up and start putting it to practice. You'll love it (you being your WHOLE you - body, mind and spirit)

9. Get Creative. Sometimes we get stuck in the left-brain side of our life. The left brain side is quite analytical. It overanalyzes, dissects, separates and compares - constantly trying to take all of the pieces apart so that it can put them back together again. If you draw or paint or write, you start tapping into your right brain. Get a bunch of folks together to do a book club on **Julia Cameron's** The Artist's Way - a spiritual approach to higher creativity. (PS: If you don't like some of the words being used, make up your own definition to those words - I find an ALPHA Poem on the word GOD: Good Orderly Direction, as she uses is quite appropriate in this sense).

10. Volunteer. Nothing feels better than giving. Give without expectation of receiving anything back, and life becomes much happier. There are plenty of organizations around the world that could use helping hands. If you find a non-profit group that you are interested in, ask them how you can help. You'll be surprised at how good it feels.

Happiness is essential to our being, and our truth of life is that deep down within we are all happy, you just have to remember how to get there. Patience, practice and persistence. Do not only choose to be happy, but practice being there over and over again.

Peace, Love and Happiness.

Write your own list of "10 things that can improve your happiness right now."

6. WHAT DOES YOGA MEAN?

Yoga: to Yoke or the noun Yoke.

The verb *yoke*, means to bring together, unite, join that which was seemingly separate to become one. The noun *yoke* is the item that connects two separate parts to become one working part - like a harness of a horse and carriage. Yoga is this whole existence of this external world, life out there, along with this whole internal world, life in here, coming together to be experienced through our Yoke, or our body.

What we are yoking in Yoga are the seemingly separate "inside world" (of thought, internal dialogue, emotion, understanding - Spirit) with this "outside world" (of experience, event, life) through the Yoke, or body, as it experiences the world out there through its sensations. The inside gets to experience the outside (and vice/versa) through this amazing instrumental tool called a human body.

The body is a sensual instrument of perception used by the spirit in deciphering the external world of life. We train it (we hope) to understand and comprehend that which is being experienced both internally and externally, through breath, awareness and presence.

From our Ego mind's point of view, we see ourselves as separate. It says we are this thing walking around in this body form taking up this space, completely separate from this existence in our external surroundings.

What yoga teaches us is that this internal and external world exist mutually, not separately, and that life is experienced through the body, presently. So what we're yoking is this experience of internal and external - we are yoking through the body.

Our natural state of existence is perfect harmony and balance. But our untrained mind perspective is to throw all this "stuff" in our way to keep us from experiencing this. (oh thank you Ego for your creative existence).

So our goal, our task, is to begin to understand what these obstacles are and to remove them from our source - so that our source and our external become the same flow or the same experience. That way you are creating your experience at the same exact time you are experiencing it, and in this there is no conflict. It's just a continual flow. Yes, we know you get it, conceptually, but you have to PRACTICE, with patience and persistence!

When we move out of the space of the present creative, we get trapped into the mind of "past and future," where life does not exist. Life exists in the present moment. It is a continuous process of change, unfolding moment, by moment, by moment. We have trained ourselves to be cut off from that experience because we're projecting what we want, and we're thinking about what happened in the past and we're worried about what's going to happen in the future. We're constantly torn away from the experience of present life. There is a lot of stress and chaos in the wandering mind. It is not a calm and quiet experience. When you experience present moment, all that pain and suffering associated with mind disappears. It's not experienced anymore. It's simply free in the observational awareness of the sensational flow of existence as it occurs. Constant change!

Do not label sensations as "like" or "dislike." They are just things that are passing through the body in any given moment. Arising and passing away, moment by moment, coming up and going away in constant change. It is our attachment to the sensation, the story we hold about it, the aversion we have to it or the fear we have of it, and the unawareness of the process that create our experience of chaos and misery.

Cultivate: Patience, Practice and Persistence

7. YOGA AND REPRESSED EMOTIONS

Yoga practices often open up blocked energies of repressed emotions. This energy could be childhood ghosts and adult unawares that we never had the opportunity to deal with. These suppressed emotions do not just disappear, but get locked into the energetic body as repressed emotions. These blocked energies, over time, can then manifest themselves as physical ailments. When we practice yoga, the postures are not only designed to limber and loosen the body, but they are also ways of releasing stored energies.

For example, when we start to clear the mind and move deeply into a yoga asana (posture) practice, we can find ourselves in a completely relaxed position, then out of no where comes that ghost and we instantly feel the entire emotion sweep upon us. It can be quite a shock. Not having thought about something for a long time, or having repressed it so much that we blocked it out of our memory, then seeing it face-to-face again can be overwhelming. What we want to do is allow the emotion to be released. Crying, anger, sweat, cold, and pain can all be a part of this emotional release. These are the Kleshas (root causes of our suffering) coming up and releasing.

Although it may seem at first that this is a negative thing happening to us, reliving an experience we didn't want to have, it is a positive thing, for this emotion is finally getting a chance to be released. We no longer need to hold onto it. If we can allow ourselves to be a witness to the emotion, let it happen without interaction from the mind or reaction from the body, then this emotion can release itself and we can be free of it.

Pain, emotional or physical, is not something we want to deal with. It is "not pleasant." Typically when we have something painful happening to us, we put our hand out and say, "NO, I will not experience this." This is the beginning of the repressed emotion. This emotion does not go away. It is simply pushed aside/inside. The energy of this emotion finds a spot in the physical body to hang out and make a home. Over time, these energies move through the body and can manifest themselves as physical dis-ease.

When these emotions/ailments come to the surface, we have two options. We can repress the emotion/ailment again, or experience it to move through us so that we can step through the other side, free of it. The ego typically has an attachment to the experience of pain. We have such an aversion to it, that we actually teach ourselves to become the victim of it, which then in turn gives us more "attention." We get attention by talking about it (remember our discussion in The Pen is Mightier Than the Sword chapter). If I can get you to feel bad about my pain, then I have created a sense of story, which helps me to be the victim, which then in turn creates more story, which helps me get attention. It is a continuous cycle. It is this craving for attention that keeps the mind attached to the experience of the sensation.

Yoga helps us to experience the pain as a witness. We get to watch it happen without reacting to it. Typically, emotion feeds a thought, which in turns intensifies the emotion, which then feeds a thought. Thus the cycle continues. As a witness to the emotion, the ego starts to silence. If we can allow ourselves the experience of the emotion without interaction or repressing it, then the emotion will not be allowed to manifest itself in the body as energy and cause future physical ailment.

Remember, we are not the thought. We are not the pain or the emotion. Our mind uses our bodily senses as a tool to connect us to the world. Our mind is the translator of the senses to the spirit. Our spirit resides in the body. Life is meant to be experienced, the good and the bad, the pleasant and the painful. It is about balance.
Experiencing all. Yoga is a tool to the balance. It helps us to experience all that is by being the center of both "good" and "bad" experience. In this place, we are content.

"We are not human beings experiencing a spiritual life. We are spiritual beings experiencing a human life."

Who do you need to forgive? Can you write them a letter talking about why you need to forgive them, even if you do not end up sending the letter? Get it out, explore it.

8. FALL IN LOVE AGAIN

A walk through Paris at night with the city lights shining over the Champs Elysees. A gondola ride down one of the Venice canals. A stroll along the cliff-side in Santorini. The full moon rising over a quiet mountain top. A night at home with a recipe book and some classic Ray Charles blues. No matter what the external experience is, spend some time rediscovering the subtlest moment of your existence, what you feel inside.

Go on a date with yourself. It doesn't have to be a foreign country, it can simply be an evening in with your favorite food, music and a journal. (Notice how I didn't say television or movie or computer?) We spend so much of our time looking to fill our "Love Bucket" with things in the external world. Dating, purchasing, watching movies, reading, facebooking, etc., all lead our mind outside of our selves to some random stimulus that we label as "love." Pick a night next week and slow it all down. Pick a night to rediscover who you are.

I've recently returned from a 10 day silent meditation. It was a wonderful experience. Ten days of not having to respond to anyone else's needs. Ten days of discovering who I truly am. You don't need ten days to discover the beauty you have within you, but you do need a few moments. The ten day meditation reminded me that I'm here to walk on my path, discover my adventures and share my journey. Maybe others have walked the path before me, but it is up to me only to take the steps forward.

As much as you can, shut off the "having to do for others" mode and do for just you. Make the dinner YOU want, without taking anyone else into consideration. Plan a night for something you want to do, because you can. It's not selfish. After all, whose life are you living?

We get so caught up in thinking that we need to make other people happy. Secretly, I believe, that when we get stuck there, it's because we hope that other people will make us happy. That will never work. Imagine the responsibility on someone else's shoulders to provide you with all the happiness you need. Imagine having that responsibility for someone else? Yeah, it still doesn't work. The only person we can truly make happy is ourselves. So work on it. Practice it. Do it because you have the choice to do so.

One thing you may want to consider practicing for yourself is forgiveness. Forgiveness is one of those things that we often think we have to do for others, or others "should" do for us. But there is a component we often forget. This is our own forgiveness of ourselves. We hold so tightly to a story of some 'thing' that happened once upon a time ago, and 10 years later we realize that we've been torturing our loving self every day because of it. Hey, you know, people mess up. They do things they probably shouldn't. Maybe they didn't know any different. Maybe we didn't either. Forgiveness comes first by forgiving the story we've created and held on to about another person or event. Then we can forgive the event/person. Forgiveness lifts a heavy heart.

Story Time: Two monks were walking through the woods (no, it's not a joke), and they came across a maiden who was attempting to cross a muddy path. She didn't want to get covered in mud. The elder monk carried the girl across the path. This is something the monks typically would not do, and it caused a great disturbance to the younger monk. Hours later, the two monks arrived at their destination, and the younger monk couldn't hold it in any longer. He asked, "Master, why did you carry that girl across the path, we are not supposed to do that." The master smiled and simply said, "Young Monk, I carried that girl for thirty seconds, you've carried the story for five hours, how much longer will you carry the burden?"

Delicious, right? It's okay, you can take a few breaths here and feel your existence. You are loved, and forgiven by that person who sees you in your mirror.

Another practice to put into your existence is loving-kindness. This is so important. Our mind is a tyrant of negativity. When we enable this negative behavior we are completely damaging our equanimity (and others). We've heard it a million different ways, "Treat others how you want to be treated." Do this not only on the physical and verbal level, but on the emotional and thought level too. If you spend the majority of your time thinking negatively of others, you have to remember, it's YOUR time and YOUR negative thought. Practice this with all things, animals, those icky bugs, plants, the Earth, your environment and yourself.

Understand how much of an impact this will have on your happiness and the love you have for yourself. Catch yourself when you think negatively about someone/something else. Have forgiveness for yourself if you realize you've been thoughtfully trashing someone else's existence. I believe in you. Practice believing in yourself.

Take care of yourself, and as you learn to do this, you will notice that the "world" takes care of itself. It has to match. That's how powerful you are. You're an ingenious self-creating guru. Just remember to create peace. Inner-peace, that's where external peace comes from. Create a love for yourself that's so deep, your "Love bucket" will fill up completely and spill out all over the place for everyone else to enjoy. You can do it. I know you can.

Write a love letter to yourself and sign it "your secret admirer". Then stick it in an envelope and mail it to yourself.

9. LOVING YOU IS EASY, BECAUSE I LOVE ME

Continue to cultivate this practice of self-nurture, care and love. As you grow to understand the importance of love for your own being, you can then begin to share the love you've been growing with others.

Think of love inside of you like a container. An empty container that is waiting to fill itself up and overflow. Once you fill your own container of love to the top it begins to overflow and people around you begin to feel this sense of love as well.

In Buddhism, there is a special practice called Metta. This is an intentional practice that a meditator will do. It is the practice of "loving-kindness, friendliness, amity, good will, kindness, love, sympathy and an active interest in others." (wiki)

The practice of loving-kindness cannot be underestimated and it is certainly not limited to one sect or religious viewpoint - in fact it is Universal. The law of Karma says that what we put out into the Universe, the Universe returns. In a Wiccan belief system, what you put out returns to you 3x over! In Christianity, what a man sows, so he reaps. Regardless of your belief, you will no doubt have experienced this.

When you put out anger, fear, frustration, greed, hatred, lust, and other negative emotional forces, you receive them back. You typically blame others when you receive it back and unfortunately the cycle continues. It puts you on the defense against that which does not feel good, but that which you created. If you practice Metta, loving-kindness, you will notice a change in your external environment. It will become less hostile and so will you in return. You will become less afraid of it. You will grow to love and nurture it more. You will look forward to your experiences and adventures. You will begin to notice that what you see in your external, is just a glimpse of what your true existence is internally (Mirror/Mirror).

The practice of Metta is a practice of loving-kindness to all sentient beings, or all beings with consciousness, or all life itself. It is understanding that the Law of Nature is the law of arising and passing away. It says that everything in the Universe has a cycle of life, arise and pass. This can be seen by looking at a whole life, or the life of a breath, or the life of a sensation on your body. It is everywhere. Something starts, then it stops. When you see life in this aspect of arise and pass, you begin to understand the value of life itself. Remember how limited your time is in this life and begin to hold a love for the process and an honor to all things that hold life. When you begin to practice this, you feel what it is to be in this process of arising and passing, and life takes on new meaning.

What you begin to experience is the *Art of Living*, as taught by SN Goenka in the Vipassana Meditation courses: To live presently and fully with love and compassion for others. You begin to live a life of meaning instead of searching for the meaning of life all the while blaming others for you not having the life you wish you had. It is so important to practice loving kindness to others. It is this practice that shows you the value of your own life. A life which is often taken for granted, a life missed out on completely because so much of your time is spent in thought dreaming up the life you yearn for, while being completely resentful of the life that you're forgetting to experience.

Be aware of what you put out to your environment in which you experience life, not just physically, but mentally and emotionally as well. Are you putting out emotions that are full of fear, doubt, anxiety, anger, resentment, guilt, frustration? First you think, then you react emotionally, then you react verbally and physically. Be aware of feeding your bodily sensations with negative thinking behavior patterns. Are you constantly reacting to aches and pains or small little things with great energy? Recognize in yourself that you do this, then practice observing without creating story. This will lead you to the present moment where you can start to cultivate feelings of compassion and love for yourself. When you accomplish this, you can practice creating peace and love for others. If we do not bring ourselves to this as a society we will fail, and we will all be blaming that failure on anyone but our own self.

Creating war to get to peace is never the answer. Be mindful of the hate you put out, whether or not you label it as teasing, making fun or joking. Hatred in the form of a joke is still hatred. Choose love always. The answer to peace is, and always will be, peace. It must start within. It must come from you. It can come from no other.

The world is in such a scary time. We are in a time that future histories will look back to as a pinnacle to their future or a failure of their past. You are the one that can make the difference.

I wish you peace. Be Happy.

Who are the most influential people in your life? Call one of them tomorrow..

10. BODY

How much time are you spending lounging around? I tell my clients to recycle THREE things - their microwave, the TV and the couch. Give them to a friend, or give them to good-will, it doesn't matter, but all three of them can go away. Don't want to give them away? Are you attached to your TV? Try going for 30 days without it. Just hand over the cable-box for 30 days, or ask your cable company to turn you off for 30 days. A cable television vacation (Yes Please, and Thank You).

If you're unwilling to part with your mind-altering television, try sitting on the floor instead of the couch. Sitting on the floor will give you the opportunity to stretch and move around and it's much better for your back. Plus you're more likely to lay back and do some crunches instead of sitting back eating a pint of Ben & Jerry's. Who knows - maybe you'll even roll over and do 10 pushups at each of the commercial breaks. I hear there are at least 10 commercials in an hour long program - that's 100 pushups. You could also march in place, do kicks, knee lifts, hamstring curls and arm raises. The options are endless, are you?

If you're a chronic internet surfer, try not turning on your computer (or smart phone) one day (what?? a day without my connection to the world??) The internet can be a fat-ass builder. There are so many wonderful distractions on it! We go on with the intention of "checking email," then four hours later we get up to go pee. If you take a day off from the computer, you're more apt to do something else. Try planting a plant in the yard or weeding. Get in touch with the Earth again. Get your hands dirty. Remember to take stretching breaks and drink lots of water. If you don't have a garden of your own, ask me! I've got PLENTY of stuff to do around the yard, and it's always fun to have company.

Beware of fat season. Yes, from the end of October through the month of February we are bombarded by candies, cakes, cookies and pies. We get them from work, from home, from friends and parties, and we eat eat eat. It's all fine and dandy until we realize that we've gained five pounds. Get moving. Go for walks at lunch, go for walks after dinner. It doesn't take much, but it takes SOMETHING. Get going. Dig out your pair of sneakers from the back of the closet and get moving. Even if it's a stroll around the neighborhood. You can play "I Spy." It is decorating season after all, and there are plenty of interestingly decorated houses in the neighborhoods.

Did you know that the more physically active you are, the less stress you have? All that sitting around leaves a LOT of extra time for the mind to think and over-analyze. If you find that you have absolutely no motivation, then hire a personal trainer. You don't have to make a life-long commitment on the spot (please, if you can hardly get off the couch, the commitment would be traumatic). But you can make a commitment for 3 sessions. A personal trainer can help you get moving. They are a motivating force, and if you have to be somewhere to meet them, you will get off your butt and go. There is a myth of affordability when it comes to training - if you turned your cable off for 30 days, you'd save enough money to hire a trainer for that time period. I offer a 3 sessions for $99.00 introductory package - that's $3.00/day for the month. Ask what certification your potential trainer has, and see if it is nationally recognized. There are a lot of gyms that train people to be trainers, but have no accredited program associated with them. Be aware of the risk when working with one of these trainers (lack of education and potential for injury).

So, this season, make a vow to get moving. Get your friends and family involved. It's much easier to get going on a walk when you have someone else with you. Don't be afraid to start. The hardest part about anything is the first step, then it's easy! Switch out your "diet coke" for a water, turn off the television, shut off the computer monitor, put on your sneakers and get moving.

Buh-Bye!

Go for a 20 minute walk every evening this week.

11. WORKING OUT

Exercise for some of us can feel like torture. Even the name "exercise" sounds like a job and there is always something *else* to do other than get the body moving and the mind calm. It is important for us to keep the body and mind in good health. A healthier body leads to a healthier mind and the combination of both leads to a more centered existence that is happier. We have such a limited amount of time to experience this very human existence, yet we are spending so much of it disconnected completely from the experience of our bodies, "living" mostly in the mind.

What is it that we don't like about getting the body moving? Is it the "pain" of it? We tend to be quick to label anything outside of our comfort zone as pain, and if we're experiencing that "pain" then our mind says we need to stop. It is important for us to remember that when we were first inhabiting this planet we didn't have desks, beds, cars, TV's, or other worldly comforts. These comforts have trained us to become quite lazy and very "comfortable." Spend a month getting the body out of its comfort zone.

The other thing to work out is the mind. The mind and body work opposite really. We need to move the body in order to get it worked out, but we typically want to keep it still because it "feels" better. The opposite is true for the mind. In order to work it out, we need to practice making it still, which is exactly what it does not want (talk about going out of the comfort zone). Stilling the mind is as simple as becoming the observer of your senses. This can be a five-minute practice each day.

Motivation
If you lack the motivation to get to the body moving, then try one of these:

Find a partner: A workout partner will be someone who you can work with at the gym or can plan to meet at a hiking spot or other destination. You'll want to find someone who you think has a little more motivation than you do but is around the same fitness level. You can take turns planning out the workouts. Knowing what you do before you get to where you're going is a key part of the program. Showing up is another. If you plan to go to the gym three days a week, then split the body workouts into three days as well, and know what you are going to do before you get there.

Find a team: Joining a sports team can be a wonderful experience. You will be with a group of people who like to do their sport and you know they'll show up for their practices. It's like joining a personal workout group which can focus on many things from swimming and rugby to yoga and hiking. Kickball anyone?

Hire a fitness guru: Hiring someone to show you what to do and how to do it can be very motivational as well. If you have not worked out at the gym, but want to learn how, then a personal trainer can help you get started and teach you proper form.

Watch a video: Commit (yes, that's a big word) to a few weeks of working out at home using a video. There are PLENTY of workout videos in existence from yoga, body weight training, and full body workouts. Make sure you start slow! Honor your body.

Take a Course: Take a yoga teacher training course. You do not have to become a teacher afterwards, but you'll get some great guidance on how to do a home practice or lead your friends in a group. Become a personal trainer. Take a course on meditation. Really. Do you think you're tough? Try a 10 day Silent meditation. www.dhamma.org I double-downward-dog dare ya!

Change it up: If you've been doing the same routine for the past 5 years, it's time to do something different. The body gets used to repetitive movement, so if you're doing the same thing over and over again, after a period of time the body isn't getting the same benefits. Plus when you're doing the same thing, the mind gets another opportunity to "check out" of the experience. Change is constant and when we follow that law with our bodies, we find that it changes along rather well. It doesn't take much, but it takes something.

Remember that life is an experience, and if you attempt to see the positive in the experiences, then you'll find yourself happier. The mind is very quick to begin negative thinking as soon as something good happens. Practice thinking good thoughts. If you notice yourself thinking "yeah but," all over the place, then make it a practice to change that habit. It takes a little practice to be happy, but it's the practice of being happy that brings happiness to you.

Do 20 pushups a day for 20 days. If you are unable to do them on the floor, do them on an angle by putting your hands on the countertop or your desk.

12. YOGA, FOR ATHLETES (AND THE REST OF US TOO)

Yoga is great for athletes. Yoga teaches our bodies and minds how to relax under strain and pressure, to be calm within chaos, to be perfectly at ease and centered when the world is spinning around you. It also gives us an awareness of our bodies and our surroundings.

The Asana – yoga poses – are a way to cleanse and detoxify the muscles. They are also used to lengthen the muscles through stretching. Athletes can have a build-up of toxin in their muscular system. Lactic acid buildup can affect our ability to perform. Tight muscles keep us from being agile and limber. The yoga poses help us to relax and release the muscles. They also help to bring fresh oxygen to the muscles after a long practice or hard game. Athletes should be able to touch their toes. Being inflexible brings us closer to injury. The poses also teach us to have comfortable and steady breath no matter what the body is doing. When the breath is comfortable and steady, the mind is too; when the mind is steady, it is more focused, which makes for a stronger game.

Another thing the poses do for us is strengthen our core. We hear it everywhere, "Strengthen your core," but what does it actually mean? Take your index finger and put it on your belly button, then let the rest of your fingers line up touching down towards your pubic bone. The spot where your pinky finger lands, that's the spot. The center of your physical core - pull it in. Feel it move in towards the spine and up towards the ribcage. This is the magic button. If your movements come from this position, they will always line up. Try it when you go bowling next.

Create a breath awareness:
If you can create a breath awareness, a moment of complete focus where the only thing your mind is concentrating on is the breath as it is coming and as it is going out, you can instantly change your game in just that one breath. Creating a breath awareness teaches you how to create an active focus on anything that you want to focus on. It gives you back your "choice."

Remember, these are just tools. In order for them to work, you must put them into practice.

Training Time

What you'll need: a timer and a comfortable, uncluttered, quiet place to sit.

How long: 5 minutes a day minimum.

The Training: Find a comfortable sitting position. Then tell yourself you will not move anything until the training is over. Set the timer for 5 minutes and then close the eyes. Be Still. Focus solely on the breath as it comes in and out of the body. Focus on the part of the breath that is most prominent for you. Maybe it's the area around the nostrils; maybe it's the area of the chest or abdomen. When you notice the mind wandering, bring the awareness back to breathing again and again.

The Challenge: Can you focus on one complete cycle of breath without the mind wandering? Can you do this for the full 5 minutes? 10 minutes? 30 minutes?

A Clue: The job of the mind, the Ego mind, is to distract you and take you away from your goal. The Ego mind will tell you that you aren't capable; it will tell you that you do not like what you're doing; it will tell you that you're not good enough; it will say that you are uncomfortable and need to move or adjust. It is always testing you to see if it can pull you away from the task. If you can create a breath awareness with a focused mind, you can begin to overcome the ego mind's constant distractions, and your game will improve dramatically.

Focus

"WILL YOU JUST FOCUS???" We hear from our coaches and teammates that we need to focus, yet, there are some days where the mind is constantly eluding us. We make a mistake, we lose our pace, and the mind starts to tell us that we're not good enough, not strong enough. It's dwelling on the he said/she said event that happened sometime other than the now. That negative flow can be instantly changed and turned around in a single breath. Breath is everything. In swimming our strokes revolve around the breath. In cycling, breath can be used as a tool for keeping pace. In throwing or hitting a ball, a breath in can be used to narrow the focus of awareness to a single point, the breath out can be used to perform an action.

A focused mind is a mind with minimal chatter in thought. A focused mind equals a focused target. The easiest object to focus on is our breath. Our breath is always with us, so we can always practice our focus on it.

Creating a breath awareness also creates a self-awareness. If we are aware of our breath, we become aware of our self. In this, we also become aware of our body. We are typically a mind-oriented society. We focus our attention to our thoughts and the stimulation of our thoughts. Athletes can have a multi-perspective because they are also focusing their attention to the improvement of their bodies to carry them throughout their sport. They train themselves by repetition and understanding. Imagine if you can understand the power of the mind and have a deeper sense of focus while you are learning a new technique. The process of learning becomes much faster. If we are unaware of our process, or our body, then our body can get out of our control without us noticing. The more we can witness, the quicker we learn to stay in mental and physical control of our own being, at all points in time, no matter what the situation is.

Imagine the power of one focused individual. Imagine the power of one focused team, experiencing the same vibe, breathing in one unified breath. This is the basis of the rhythm, the groove. It is fundamental in sport. When it is understood, it is a tool to create power and precision.

Consider joining a sports team. One of the cool things about joining a new sports endeavored group, besides all the fantastic people you'll meet - is all the cool gear you collect to participate. You can look for deals for sporting goods on places like Craigslist.org. I also like to ask my friends as most of them have some sort of dust covered equipment hiding out in their garages.

PS: The same techniques can work for all you corporate gurus with your team of employees.

Sit in absolute stillness for 15 minutes a day.

13. SPRING CLEANING

During springtime, when you make your way around the city, you may notice there is a lot of change going on. Trees are budding, flowers are blooming and the sunshine stays with us a bit longer each day. It is the beginning of Spring. It is the time of year when nature is refreshing herself, so it is a perfect opportunity for us to follow her lead.

We're entering a time in our human existence when what once was considered valuable is no longer serving us. The time of "I want what I want, and I want it now" is starting to move aside, and a new generation of awareness is strongly coming into existence. We are finding that more people are letting go of the concept of immediate gratification, knowing that they are perfect exactly where they are. As we enter this new existence, notice where your conflicts are. What are the true causes of your suffering? If you cannot figure it out, maybe it's time to simplify. This is where we follow Mother Nature for some Spring cleaning.

If you have a dirty body, you will have a dirty mind. A dirty body extends far beyond just taking a shower. There are a handful of very easy-to-do cleanses for the body that will help to cleanse the mind and the energies of the body in the process. It is cleaning out the filter systems that naturally exist within the body.

Clean your mouth. Our mouth is like a toxic waste dump. Our saliva does a pretty good job of maintaining some basis of health, but with all of the junk that we chew on during the day, it cannot possibly keep up with us. It is important to properly clean the mouth. One way to do this is a gum and tooth cleanse. This is very simple to do. You will need a natural salt and a natural oil (sesame oil works great). You take a few pinches of salt and a few drops of oil and mix them to create a paste. Then you take a pinch of the mixture with your fingers and massage the teeth and gums. Spit out the excess and rinse the mouth with warm water.

Cleaning the teeth this way is natural. The salt and oil do not have the extra added chemicals that most toothpastes have, so you are not introducing foreign chemicals into your system - the mind will appreciate this. The salt will draw away the excess bacteria in the mouth and scour the teeth while the oil lubricates the gums. Some toothpastes have alcohol in their product which dries out the gums, creating potential future problems.

Next, clean the tongue with a tongue scraper. This is a device you can find in most health sections of the stores. It is a U-shaped device that you place at the back of your tongue, press down and draw it forward, scraping the bacteria and toxins off of the tongue. It is not enough to just brush the tongue with an already dirty toothbrush, you must scrape it to remove the excess toxin. The less toxin in the body, the less toxin in the mind. If you cannot afford a tongue scraper, the back of a teaspoon works just fine.

Now that the mouth is clean and clear, we need to **clean out the sinuses**. The sinuses are the gateway for our breath. Our breath is the giver of our life: without it, we do not exist here. It is important to clear out the nasal passages and sinus cavity. To do this we practice Jala Neti, or Nasal Cleansing. You will need a neti pot, or you can use a glass of water and your hand.

Fill a neti pot with warm salted water. I find that a half-teaspoon of salt with two cups of warm water work fine. The water needs to be warm, not hot. The spout of the neti pot is placed into one nostril and then the head is tilted to the side, chin towards the shoulder. The salted water will run up one nasal passage, go through the sinus cavity and flow out the other. The salt draws out the bacteria and excess junk, while the water irrigates the passage itself. If you are not using a neti pot, then pour a little of the salted water into your cupped hand and gently sniff the water into your sinus cavity. This way is a little more difficult, and you may swallow a bit more water, but it is still effective.

Once you irrigate both nostrils, you need to spend a few minutes gently blowing the excess water out. Place your finger on your right nostril and blow *gently* out the left 20 times, then switch nostrils, then do it with both nostrils open. Finally, stand up, take a breath in and as the breath comes out (through the nose) bend forward dropping the chin by the chest. This will get the rest of the water out. I find this practice is done best outdoors, but a shower also works if you have room in it.

(There is a new product on the market that is like a squeegee bottle. I do not recommend this. It creates a pressure in the ear canals and forces water into places it should not go.)

Clean your food. Eat food that is natural and not junk. Again, what you put into your body affects your mind. If you eat junk food, fatty food, processed food, five cups of coffee, meat, cookies, chips, cakes, cigarettes, alcohol, drugs and more, then expect to have a chaotic mind. Seriously! These products create negative and chaotic thinking in the mind. Changing what you put into your body will change the processing in your mind.

Clean your mouth again - this is what is coming out of the mouth. Stop the gossip, judgments, banter, and negative energy that comes out of the mouth. It's not easy if you're used to it, but if you want to be free of the daily butt-kickings from the over-active mind, then you have to practice not spitting it out. Shutting off the television will give your mind a break and stop overloading it with garbage, anxiety, and judgement. The less that goes in, the less that comes out.

Finally, **clean your environment**. Pick up your home, your room, your clutter, your desk, your bathroom, your vehicle, and clean them. A wiping down with water and vinegar and a cloth is just fine really. Change and wash your bed sheets and wipe down your mattress. Once you get going, it gets done quickly.

Denny Richard

Give yourself a hug, take a few deep breaths and know that no matter how chaotic it seems, everything is going to be absolutely okay. Spring cleaning is an opportunity. It is a fresh start, a new perspective, a glimpse at a different life. If you feel like dancing, or singing, or acting like a goof because it breaks you out of your shell, then do it. Have fun.

Today I choose to be Happy

14. BALANCE

Balance, from this to that, from the Out to the In, is a constant ebb and flow of opposites. When we observe this process without reaction, life becomes as calm and clear as a wooded lake. It is also important to bring into your body and environment things that will help to create balance. When we practice moderation, whether it be with a food, drink, or other substance, then the physical, energetic and mental bodies will begin to find their ways back into balance.

Have you ever had the experience where you've ingested too much of a substance? You may have noticed that shortly thereafter your body physically becomes out of balance. Too much coffee will make the body jittery and tense and the mind chaotic; too much alcohol will make the body sloppy and the mind depressive, and too much junk food will make the body heavy and the mind dull. The energetics of the body change as well. After all since everything is made of energy (including food), then the fuel you are supplying to your body has a great impact on how the body and mind will feel, not only physically, but energetically and emotionally. Excess stimulants create an over-stimulated mind; excess depressants create a mind that automatically responds in a negative manner. This isn't rocket science, but somehow we conveniently "forget."

It doesn't take much to bring your entire existence into balance, but it does take a little practice and, yes, "work." You actually have to want to be in balance to get there. This means not drinking the whole pot of coffee, but possibly limiting or even eliminating your intake. If you favor an alcoholic beverage at the end of a day, have one instead of three, or even have a day where you drink nothing but water. Water, in itself, is already balanced.

We've all heard of Karma, and when we practice eliminating Karma we also find that we come more into balance. That practice is the non-reactive practice. It is a practice of observation. What we may say is, "Well, how do I get anything done if I don't react?" What happens is when we observe the current moment, the chatter box mind gets out of the way and you start to connect to your source of inspiration. When you connect to this source you are inspired and begin to take conscious action. There is such a struggle in the mind to allow this to happen. When you're not sure what to do next, just start observing what is now. The "what comes next" will start to arrive automatically. Then you will be inspired and begin to do just that.

The physical practice of yoga, the poses and postures that you see, are partially designed to create balance in the body (both physical and energetic). The movements, along with breath and awareness, help you to find that centered space within you. This is the space that can participate as the observer of this "outer world" that we see, and the "inner world" that we imagine. This is the space between here and there. With practice you can locate this space and begin the process of observation in both directions.

If you're feeling mentally imbalanced, scatter brained, "ADD-minded," etc., try balancing poses. Stand on one leg and attempt to balance. The mind and the body are closely related (although some of us have forgotten this). If you are attempting to physically and literally balance with your body, your mind will have to follow, otherwise you will wobble and fall over.

Your external environment also has a huge effect on your internal balance system. If you are surrounded by chaos and disorder, then the mind will be overstimulated with this as well. This will create an energetic imbalance, and since everything is connected, eventually your body will catch up. Find ways to organize and simplify. It may seem a daunting task if you haven't done so, but it can be fun and easy. Start with grouping things together and cleaning them. Then find spaces to stick your groups of items OR find places to donate them. Getting rid of the excess is another way to bring your experience to a more balanced one. After all, too much of a thing is just too much. Does it seem a bit overwhelming to start without help? Try the Fly Lady (www.flylady.net).

Clean your environments.

15. CHANGE

Tuesday morning you wake up and you yearn for change. You want something to be different. Then Thursday comes along and you're petrified because all that change you've been longing for starts coming and you cannot escape it.

Change is inevitable, right? Everything is constantly shifting and changing in each and every moment, yet somehow our brains have programmed us to fight it! When we allow ourselves to surrender to what is, we move directly into the flow of change. That means accepting the "good" as well as the "bad." In this acceptance we let go of the "control" of our lives. We tend to think that we're in control, but it is a false reality, a delusional thought process in an attempt to create harmony out of what the mind otherwise labels as chaos.

We usually recognize change when we realize that something we have been experiencing is coming to an end. Whether it be a relationship, a job, or a yoga class. Every ending is also a beginning. Do you find yourself in anxiety about where you will be tomorrow? We may say we're afraid of change, but it is most likely that we are anxious about what we do not know of what is yet to come. Accepting the anxiety and being with the emotion, instead of fretting about what you do not yet know, will allow you to move through change with ease.

Pay attention to the stories that are created by the mind. Everyone in our life is here to teach us. We learn from everyone at all times. Some of the lessons are easy, some not so. The mind is a powerful thing: it is our best friend, but also our worst enemy. The mind creates stories based on emotions and sensations. These stories aren't "real," they are just there, kind of like clouds floating by. We experience them as real because we have emotions that react to the thoughts that pass through the mind. The stronger the thought, the stronger the emotion and the sense that the thought is real. Since we experience the emotion and feel it, we assume that the thoughts associated with them are real.

If you put it into your mind that someone has wronged you, you continue to build new thoughts based on the initial feeling. Then the emotions you experience because of these thoughts will feed the thoughts, and the cycle of thought and emotion will continue. The reverse is also true: If you put it into your mind that you are attracted to someone, then no matter what they do, you will continually see them in the positive. This will feed those same attraction emotions, which create more thoughts and make for a continuous cycle. This whole process is constantly changing from one moment to another. Our minds do not recognize that it is changing. Our mind sees only cycle, because it bases it's existence purely on Past and Future.

The practice of yoga teaches us to find peace within our minds. This peace comes from observation of the deepest places within, and these places show us our clearest path. Our intuition becomes more in tune, and we are able to make choices from a place of clarity rather than a place of confusion. The place that we touch upon inside of us when we practice yoga is neither up nor down, or wrong nor right. It just is - as is change. When we practice being with this place we let go of the suffering caused by the mind. Patanjali's sage advice tells us: "Heyam Dukham Anagatam" - "The suffering which has not yet come can and should be avoided." (II 16) This suffering stuff, yeah, we do it to ourselves.

Give yourself a hug. A long, slow deep breathed hug that lasts for more than 10 seconds. It's OK, I love you.

16. NUTRITION
IT ISN'T EASY BEING GREEN

(Caution: When Denny gets overly passionate about things, he sometimes cusses - there may be a few cuss words in this next section - just sayin.)

A few years back I started to learn about how what we do with our external environment has a direct effect on our internal environment, and the more I learned, the more I was horrified at what we were doing.

The healthcare and health insurance/prescription drug companies in the world are the wealthiest companies out there, because WE are unhealthy almost constantly. Why?

Products surround us like the stars fill the sky, and we are quick to grab onto whatever trendy item society deems fashionable, without really understanding the true "cost" of what that product does. For YEARS, we've been told how important it is to cover our bodies with sunscreen, and for years we've been doing just that. However, most of the product that we're covering our bodies with is just as toxic as the sun. Most large corporations do not use organic materials, and we buy whatever the Big Businesses (*BB*) tell us is appropriate. Those products are typically full of chemicals, chemicals which themselves cause cancer when introduced to the body. So here we are, lathering up cancer onto our skin to protect our skin from the cancer causing Sun. Does that piss you off as much as it does me? I hope so. Here's a hint for what products you might want to put on your body - **if you wouldn't EAT it, don't lather it up on your skin.** Also, wearing organic fabrics are better for the skin. Cotton, bamboo, hemp and wool are better for you and the environment.

Beauty products should have a shelf life like food, albeit a little bit longer. So, that florescent yellow cancer causing sunscreen you got from the big isle of the blue light special store is not what you want to use. Go to a local farmer's market and ask the product people there how they make their goods. There are plenty of folk that make their body care products fresh from their gardens. **Yes, Please!**

We can apply this principle to cleaning products as well. If you need to wear a mask and gloves to clean your house with the products you have purchased, then you're just adding more toxicity to your environment. There are an abundance of wonderful green-clean products available that clean your house better than toxic chemical. If you want to wash your floors with bright purple liquid, you might want to put your baby in a hazardous materials suit before placing them on the ground. That floor is NOT clean, it's toxic. Remember, don't believe anything I tell you, but Big Business (*BB*) = Big Trouble. Remember, *BB* once told us that smoking was good for us and that asbestos was a great product. Were they right? You could always make your own cleaning products, and it's much easier than you might think!

Shop local for your products. Buy from local vendors who use nature to create their products. Shopping local also means that the money you're spending on your product stays in your community. When you shop a *BB* chain, you send your money out of the state for some other to benefit from. Put your local community back to work. They will then end up supporting you in return. **Local first!**

One of my favorite subjects to talk about is food. I LOVE food. I'm a complete foodie. That is why I get items that are actual food items grown by local organic farmers. If you can get strawberries in January, that's a problem. How do you think they're grown? Most likely they've been injected with growth hormones, covered in pesticides and injected with food coloring. Tasty, huh?

Fast Food = **Fastly Failing** health. Here's the hamburger story: Hamburger, a used to be ground up cow is now pretty much anything but. Now-a-days, thanks mostly to the fast food industry, hamburgers are mostly "Filler." "Filler" is a nifty invention created by the (*BB*) Fast Food industries to help combat the contamination of meat with E. coli. You see, they're in the business of production. I don't know if you've ever driven by a mass cow slaughter house, but it's one of the most disgusting places created. Hundreds of cows packed into tiny spaces with no grass or grains to graze on. You see, *BB* has started feeding them corn, which cows can't even digest, because it's cheap! The animals are given limited shade and are standing waist deep in their own fecal matter.

Well, these cows have to be slaughtered, right, because we want our 99 cent hamburger. So, into the slaughter house goes the shit covered cow, barely hosed off (not that hosing a cow down will clean off the feces). Then the cow is slaughtered with crap flying all over the freshly corn-fed, growth hormone and antibiotic-injected slab of meat. Mmmm yummy. Well, the FDA said, "*BB* Cow Meat Company, you need to get your fecal matters under control," so instead of putting cows out to a pasture to graze on grass lands, letting nature take care of most of their problem, they contacted another *BB* company and said, "We need to kill the E. coli." So *BB* company No. 2 comes up with this "Filler," which is comprised of a cardboard-like gooey substance mostly made of ammonia. "Just mix this right in with your ground up, poop-covered, hormone-injected, antibiotic, corn-fed, mal-nutritioned cow and VOILA, mostly dead E. coli." Great - Thanks *BB* Cow Company for destroying yet another perfectly good food source.

Okay, I'll stop, for now. But I strongly suggest that you consider what it is that you're purchasing, eating, drinking and putting onto your body. It's all connected. And again, don't believe anything I said here. As far as you know I could be making it all up.

Bake something healthy (or make soup).

17. AYURVEDA 101
THE BRIEF INTRO

Ayurveda, also known as the Science of Life, is a science of self-healing. It has two main purposes. First, its aim is to keep a healthy person healthy. Second, if a person finds that they have come out of balance, its goal is to remove the imbalance by the root and bring the body, mind, spirit back into balance, where perfect health resides.

Ayurveda regards the body/mind/spirit triad as an elemental existence. It understands the composition of the body is made of elements - Earth, Air, Fire, Water and Ether. It is these combination of elements which make up our constitution, or dosha. Our Ayurvedic dosha is our guideline to a balanced Human existence. The idea is in understanding what your dosha consists of, then "feeding" it nutritionally, physically, emotionally, energetically, those things that will bring that dosha into balance and maintain it. We'll explain this further as we go along.

There are three main doshas. Vata, Pitta and Kapha. Vata type dosha is made primarily of the elements of Air and Ether. When we think of the qualities of air and ether, we think of dry, light, rough, mobile, clear, cold and subtle. Pitta type dosha is made primarily of the elements Water and Fire. Qualities of Pitta are oily, sharp, hot, light, mobile, liquid and clear. Kapha qualities, made of Earth and Water, are heavy, slow, cold, oily, slimy, dense, soft, static and cloudy.

To balance the doshas, it is important to balance the qualities of the dosha. For instance, since Kapha is made of qualities of heavy, dense, cloudy, and cold, adding more of these qualities to Kapha will create more imbalance. For those of us with obesity issues (which are the majority of Americans), we are facing an excessive Kapha imbalance. What are food/nutritional items that are Kapha? Cream, Butter, starchy foods, animals, sweet foods and veggies, dairy. Can you see how these foods are also cold, slow, dense, and cloudy? Adding cold, slow and dense to something that is already cold, slow and dense, just makes more of it, which we see manifesting in our already out of balance bodies.

To get a better understanding of how your food plays a role in your balance, you can identify food qualities by the way they taste. Astringent foods (beans, tea, apples, legumes) are Vata quality foods. Sour (citrus, yogurt, tomatoes, vinegar), Pungent (ginger, hot pepper, radish, mustard, cloves) and Bitter (green leafy veggies, beets, celery, broccoli, sprouts) foods are the quality of Pitta. Sweet (starchy, bread, pasta, rice, meat, sugar, honey) and Salty (sauces, fish, salts, soy) are Kapha quality foods.

If you are out of balance (have too much, or excessive) in one of your dosha, you would be able to recognize these symptoms being produced in the body. Excessive Vata symptoms include: Emaciation, constipation, coldness, dizziness, tremors, confusion, depression. Excessive Pitta: Fever, inflammation, hunger, thirst, insomnia, anger, burning sensations. Excessive Kapha: nausea, depression, heaviness, lethargy, chills, cough, difficulty breathing, poor digestion. Giving spicy food to an already angry person makes a person more angry. Get it?

A beautifully written book called <u>Eat, Taste, Heal - an Ayurvedic Guidebook and cookbook for Modern Living</u>, written by Thomas Yarema, MD, Daniel Rhoda, DAS and Chef Johnny Brannigan, gives us a bunch of helpful hints on a balanced way of eating:

Vata type - To create more balance favor foods with sweet, sour and salty tastes. Favor heavy, moist and warming foods. Eat fewer bitter, pungent and astringent foods. Eat smaller, regular meals three to four times per day. Eat a balanced breakfast each morning. Avoid eating when nervous or anxious. Sit down to eat and always avoid eating on the run. Eliminate white sugar and caffeine. Use warming spices to improve digestion and avoid cold and carbonated beverages.

Pitta type - Favor foods with Sweet, bitter and astringent tastes. Favor cool, dry and slightly heavy foods. Eat fewer Salty, Sour and Pungent foods. Eat at regular times each day. Eat a balanced breakfast and an early lunch. Avoid refined sugar. Limit alcohol and caffeine. Avoid conducting business while eating. Don't eat poorly just because your digestion can handle it.

Kapha type - Favor foods with bitter, pungent and astringent tastes. Favor light, dry and warming foods. Eat fewer sweet and salty foods. Eat less in quantity and frequency. Eat at regular times each day. Eat a light breakfast, eat a light evening meal. Avoid frequent snacking and late-night eating. Eliminate white sugar and greasy foods. Use warming spices to improve digestion. Favor warm beverages.

Ayurvedic principles are simple to follow. I find them much easier to understand than the ineffectual calorie counting we tend to "diet" ourselves with. Diets simply do not work. They don't actually take care of the imbalance, but leave us craving that which we do not give ourselves. Those crash diets and "miracle" programs allow us to drop weight (often too quickly). Then because we do not actually change our habits, we put it back on, plus an extra twenty pounds. How is that supposed to make us feel better?

Ayurvedic ways of eating nutritionally are not only for us over-fat folk. I use it to balance my pitta. It helps to keep my mind calm and more centered without being so reactionary in anger. Vata types need grounding - so avoiding coffee and other things that send them buzzing along life's over-paced highway is a must to keep them centered.

Life has a number of amazing tools for us to use to discover the depth of what we can truly accomplish. When you discover one of those tools, use it to sculpt the life you dream yourself to have. I don't know anyone more perfect than you that could do it better.

To find out what your dosha is consider taking a short quiz on Ayurvedic Constitution. There are plenty online. A more comprehensive way would be to meet with an Ayurvedic Practitioner.

Make a vision board: Start collecting images, words, patterns, colors of things you wish to manifest in your life and in your community. Possible Categories: Friends, Family, Travel, Education, Finance, Health, Children, Art, Career. After collecting these images for 21 days, take them out and paste them to a board. Place the board in an area where you will see it at least one time each day. Take time to sit in front of the board and feel a sense of gratitude for what you have in your life already.

18. THE FOOD WE EAT

The grocery store is an interesting place. Upon entering, you see rows upon rows of "food" stuff. If you want an instant change to getting healthy, then you'll have to shop for your food (preferably at farmer's markets) more often.

Here's a trick to shopping a grocery store – Shop the perimeter of the store. There you will find fruits and vegetables that haven't been altered (unless you're not buying organic). Fresh meats for you carnivorous folk and dairy are also found out on the edges of stores. You will also find fresh grains. The more you stick to the perimeter, the healthier the food item. "Food" that has been processed and given a shelf life of more than a few weeks is typically not a food that is providing great benefit to you.

Rediscover what food is and what it tastes like. Spend some time in a grocery store looking at food. Walk through the produce section and pick up different foods. Feel the textures, smell them. Ask the produce clerk what foods are that you do not know.

If you make it an adventure, you can also shop the local farmer's markets. Here you will find locally grown and most likely organic produce. Produce typically needs to be eaten within the first couple of weeks of harvest to receive its most abundant source of nutrition. "Dead Food" is dead nutrition. If food is on its way out, or has been excessively processed, then it is dead and does not give us any nutritional value.

Processed foods have already been broken down by machines. When we eat processed foods, we get hungry faster. Let's take flour for example. Wheat is this beautiful grain. White flour is wheat that has been broken down by a machine (pulverized), then bleached (to make it white) which strips out all the natural nutrients. What is left is white powdery "stuff." This stuff has very little nutritional value for the body. It's junk really. The body eats other *stuff* made from this *stuff* and since it is already broken down, it gets processed very quickly in the body. Not long after eating something like this we get hungry again. Why? Because the "food stuff" quickly passes through our systems, since there is nothing for our systems to do with it.

Whole grain foods are broken down by our bodies, not machines. So when we eat whole grains, we do not get as hungry as quickly. The food stays in our system for a longer time while the body does the work to break it down. Since the body is WORKING to break it down, it's also burning hotter which means that it is also breaking down excess fat to use as fuel to burn what we are eating. What IS that bright yellow "cheese" stuff they put on things like cheese puffs? If it looks like toxic waste, maybe you want to avoid putting it into your body. Most beverages should not be different shades of neon, don't you think?

Avoid Fast Food. Most fast food places do not have any interest in your health. Fast Food is not your friend. We are a fast food nation and we are also a FAT food nation. There isn't much difference between fast food and fat food. Look at how fat we've become.

(Hey Guys - want to gain an inch in length, "down there?" Lose 30 pounds! Seriously! Now that's some incentive!)

Stop drinking soda. Talk about junk!! This "stuff" is the worst. Just because the pop companies say their drink is "0 calorie" it doesn't mean it's healthy. It's still Junk! If you're looking for a flavored beverage, try an iced tea without the excess stuff in it (HINT: Make your own). The major US bottling companies put a ton of chemicals in their drinks. Their labels should really say 95% chemical, 4% water and 1% tea. They're not interested in your health, they're interested in keeping you addicted to their product so you spend your money on them. Using the excuse,

"But it's labeled DIET, so it MUST be good for me," is now completely unacceptable for you.

Avoid any foodstuff with *High Fructose Corn Syrup* on their label. Talk about bad stuff, this stuff is deadly. High Fructose Corn Syrup is a man-made concoction, a by-product of another chemical process, which was found to sweeten things. (Man-made - Imagine a scientist with a white lab coat and protective goggles and protective gloves mixing a group of chemicals under a hood in a lab... "Here, I just mixed this stuff together, drink it, it's sweet, you'll like it.")

Here's what happens and how the body reacts - When we eat a sugar, the body releases insulin to break down the sugar. When we eat a man-made sugar, the body releases insulin to break it down. But guess what, there is no "sugar" there. So the body gets confused. Since insulin gives the body a clue that it's satisfied, the lack of it being produced tells the body that it isn't satisfied. Then we overeat. Overeating leads to obesity, which can lead to Type II Diabetes (which is RAPIDLY growing, especially in the USA). Since you are training your body to release insulin to break down a "non-sugar," if it gets confused enough, it will stop releasing the insulin all-together. Because it thinks there isn't any sugar there to break down.

There are two reasons we eat – for nutrition and for pleasure. Finding the balance between these two reasons for eating will create balance within you. Overeating makes us over-fat. Believe it or not, we do not need all that much food to survive. Our egos will tell us differently of course – because the ego is addicted to craving. It loves to be fed. By telling the ego that we're not going to overfeed it, it starts to breakdown its hold on craving. Little by little it lets go of its desire to satisfy, then eating becomes something whole and new. It becomes an experience in itself!

Try eating with awareness: Pick a meal, any meal that you would typically eat, it could be just one avocado. Turn off the television (or better yet, throw it in the recycle bin), and sit in a space with minimal distraction. Sit with the avocado, feel the weight of it in your hand. Feel the texture, smell it, look at the color of it. Then take a knife and cut it open. Feel the knife in your hand and feel it slice into the avocado. Feel the impact of the blade against the seed in the center. Cut all around it. Open the avocado after it's been cut by twisting the two halves. Remove the seed in the center.

Take a moment to look at the avocado's color, observe the smell. If you'd like, you can crack some fresh pepper on top of it. Take a spoon and scoop out a small bite of the avocado. As the spoon comes to the mouth, smell the avocado and feel the sensations of the avocado passing through the lips into the mouth. Feel it against the tongue, notice the sensations created. Notice the salivary glands. Chew into the bite you've just put into your mouth. Feel the sensations of the teeth passing through the avocado. After you finish chewing, swallow the bite and notice the sensations of the fruit passing from the mouth, down the throat to the stomach. Take a breath and notice the sensations of it sitting in the stomach.

Again, spoon out another piece of the avocado and repeat the process. Notice how long it takes you to eat. Notice all the different sensations that can be related to the process of eating. It takes about 5-10 minutes for the mind to realize the body is full. If we add a television or other mindless distraction into the process of eating, that time gets closer to 20 minutes. By then, we've already overeaten.

Fast food companies make it "easy" because the foodstuff is readily available and CHEAP (Cheap being the focus). Remember, you do not need as much whole grain food to nutritionally feed the body and the body isn't as hungry after eating it, so in essence, it's less expensive to feed the body better food, and in the long run, MUCH less expensive because of the medical bills related to unhealthy eating habits.

Yes, it takes a little more effort to eat well, but it also takes a little more effort to live well. We've become so lazy and distracted by the wants of life that we forget to take the time for us. Conscious meal planning and purchasing quality food items is another way to say, "Hey, yeah I DO care about myself." If you're not going to care about yourself, no one else is. It is your life, your choice. The only one that can take care of you is YOU. Beware, and be aware of the items that you are introducing to your system. If you want to feel good, then you have to choose to feel good, and that is choosing the foods that are good for you.

Yup - You're still worth it.

Food for thought: If you eat it, you become it. Same goes for the drink. So if you're stuffing yourself with alcohol (a depressant), expect your mind to think negative thoughts. If you're stuffing yourself with fatty, dense, and heavy foods, expect your mind to become that as well - slow moving and unclear (like butter). Racy foods and drugs do just that to the mind. This is why it is so important to have a clean external environment and a clean internal environment. Being thoughtful of what you eat actually matters.

Eat more vegetarian meals this month.

19. THE IN AND THE OUT (SUMMING IT UP)

On the journey of life, we come upon many teachers. Every moment, when we are aware of it, can be a teacher of life. Teachers come in many forms and we tend to label them as good or bad, but regardless the label, it's what we get from the lesson that counts. The closest teacher you'll ever come across is yourself. What is it that you wish to learn?

If you're finding difficulties in your path, do some energy clearing. Talking about energy doesn't mean you have to create stories of zulus and witches. Energy is everything. Everything is made up of energy. Things just vibrate on different frequencies. Hot vibrates faster than cold. Clearing your energy, in your body and your environment, can clear out obstacles along your path.

In terms of the body, we are creatures of our external environment. We are what we eat - those things we put into our bodies get broken down and rebuilt as cells. We feed our bodies with foods and beverages, hopefully herbs, roots, flowers and barks along with some other grains, fruits and veggies. Some of the garbage we DO put into our bodies is not very friendly to our systems. Just because it was made by humans as "food," doesn't mean it's actually meant to be in your system. We're humans, we've made mistakes. Let's not keep remaking them. Don't believe me? Remember when we mentioned that it was thought Asbestos was a good thing and smoking was healthy? Uh huh - think of that in terms of "food." High Fructose Corn Syrup, Trans Fats, pills, those very colorful "sweetener" packets, and the list goes on.

If you can pick it from a tree and put it in your mouth, you're much closer to what food should be. Are you a meat eater? Where does your slab of meat come from? How was it treated before it was slaughtered? What was it fed? Was it injected with growth hormones or antibiotics? Were the grains it was fed dusted with pesticides? Why aren't you asking these questions? Maybe you'll start asking if cancer shows up, or maybe not. *Yeah, keep smoking those cigarettes, they're doing you great.*

To really clean out your body, you have to be very aware of what it is that you're putting into it. If you really want to change your own resonance, you have to eat foods that do not wreak havoc on your system. Eating foods with poor quality creates a poor quality body and mind. So often people complain about how much their thoughts are overwhelming, yet they drink coffee all day long, smoke cigarettes and refuse to change. You don't think that has an effect on your mentality? Have you tried going without it? *Hasn't someone created a pill for that yet?.*

Your external environment is also a direct reflection of you. If you have a room in your house that is your "avoid" room, it most likely reflects a part of you that inside may not be so great either. In Feng Shui, your home is a mirror to the parts of your life. If you've got your cat box in your love and relationship corner, and you're the type that doesn't scoop regularly, try not to be too surprised if you've got a shitty love life. Got cobwebs in your room of finance, you may find that your bank accounts reflect it as well.

Hogwash you think, eh? Well, no one can make you believe anything you don't want to believe in. But you also have the choice to believe in what you do believe in. You are a scientist and the experiment at the same time. Try cleaning out the room in your home that is the room you avoid the most, then see how different parts of your life change. If YOU do the cleaning, you'll clear your own karmic space. *Can you get right up close to your toilet bowl at this moment?*

If the first thing you do when you wake up is chug coffee, drink soda, pop a pill, smoke some dope, or continue stuffing your face with intoxicants, chances are your life is just as intoxicated. Spend a day drinking water - yeah, there's a whole new concept - Water! Here's a hint on taste in water - it's not the water that doesn't taste good, it's the toxins coming out of your tongue that don't taste good. (Except in Phoenix, I lived there 5.5 years and the water coming out of that tap was vile).

Become your own Guru. Study yourself and your environment. Make conscious change and then participate in the synchronicity.

Plant a garden, container garden, or herbs for your kitchen.

20. CONFLICT

In life's amazing journey, we encounter a variation of energy from hot to cold, black to white, rugged to smooth. Everything is vibrating with an enormous amount of energy, so great in fact that it keeps things held in place (like the gravitational pull of the sun with the planets, or the gravitational pull of an atom and its nuclei). We can see energy like we can see the ripples in the horizon as the heat is rising up towards the sky from the tarred parking lot. We can feel various forms of energy, like when we get that happy butterfly feeling in the stomach that makes you think you have to pee or throw up, right before we're about to talk to someone we find interesting.

We can also feel energy in the form of emotion. Our emotions guide us from one situation to another, sometimes blindly. When someone is walking down the street towards you, you can feel their energy. You can tell before they even get to you whether they're in a good mood or bad. If you see someone across a crowded room, and you focus all of your intent and energy on them, and as you breathe you draw their attention to yours using your own energy, they will turn and look at you (just make sure you acknowledge them before you look away).

Fun, right?

Take up the viewpoint of an observer: One who observes, pays their attention and is aware of the events unfolding as they unfold without reacting to them. It's stopping everything you're doing, and perhaps sitting down to listen to all the sounds you can hear. Inside of the spaces of sound is a silence and an amazing space of clarity.

Observation can be placed on any of our senses, and also our thoughts and emotions. Awareness and thought cannot occupy the same place, if you're aware of your own awareness, you come out of the seemingly endless cycle of thought and reaction.

What happens when we're in a relationship? Any kind of relationship with another human. More often than not, we find ourselves in conflict at one point in time.

If you find yourself in conflict, it's because *you* are reacting to a situation. When we own that reaction, we can do something about it. The reaction is typically a thought that is interpreting a sensation that may have felt similar to one that you experienced before. The reaction causes a deeper emotion, which then causes another thought. Then, that reaction causes a reaction in another, then the cycle continues and spreads. Here's a little clue - **everything is in constant change** - EVERYTHING.

Life evolves from one form to another, as does emotion and thought. Since everything is in constant change, we have to remind ourselves that just because we're feeling a similar energy, does not mean that it is the same experience. There is a big difference from when you first burned yourself on a stove to the first time you may have "accidentally" spilled candle-wax on your nipples. Though, both of the experiences involve intense heat, it is our reaction to that experience, that energy, which creates the turmoil of the mind either by ignoring it, attaching to the way you like it, fearing that it will happen again, creating an aversion to the sensation, or simply by allowing the mind to create a story around it.

The person that becomes aware of the reaction cycle can stop it by taking a breath in and focusing their attention on a sensation they are experiencing. By choosing to not play that circuit over again, you break the chain of it and can move onto something else like a different emotion, experience, thought. Close your eyes for a moment and focus all of your attention on the sensations you feel on your right big toe... go ahead, we'll wait.

You may have experienced warmth, dryness, coolness, moisture, pressure, itching, tickling, vibrational. Whatever sensation you experienced is what is happening in the current moment. Through awareness though, you have left the cycle of thought/emotion/reaction. You leaves the creative thought process, and puts yourself into the experience of what it is that is being created, the experience of life.

When you're in conflict and it's becoming an argument, allow the other person to get all of their talking out (whether or not you think them right or wrong, or whether or not you have all their answers) - let yourself begin an awareness of breath. You can still be cognizant of what is being relayed, but because you're not reacting either with words, actions, thoughts or emotions, that cycle is being broken down. Taking a breathing break doesn't have to be out of spite, but it *can* be out of love, for not only the other person, but yourself. It's okay if you do not agree, we know that life is full of disagreements. It's also okay that you have a different opinion than someone else - neither is right nor wrong. Each person is here to live their experience and their journey. We can either support them, or move out of their space. Support does not mean that you have to agree with them. Support can be that you allow them the time and space to figure out what they need to figure out and still love them for who they are while they learn what they're learning. Hopefully they will do the same for you.

It is so easy to see all the things another person has to do in order to make themselves better. But it is THEIR lesson to learn. If only it were so easy to know all of the things that would make ourselves better. By having compassion and understanding for another person's processing, we get that back in return. It is up to no one but yourself to create happiness. Create so much happiness for yourself that it fills you up and spreads to everyone that comes in contact with you. If you want to be in a "good" relationship, then be the "good" in the relationship. I can't imagine seeing a Vegan and a Butcher in a relationship with each other, but then again, the Universe has an amazing way of balancing itself.

Life is a choice, breath it in.

Who do you habitually blame for the way you are feeling? Recognize when you instantly place blame on someone else for your external life not matching your internal vibration. Start to take ownership of YOUR feelings.

21. AN OBSERVER'S GUIDE TO A HEALTHY RELATIONSHIP

Rule # 1: Remember to date yourself every once and a while. Take yourself out for dinner and a trip to the bookstore. Enjoy afternoon at a spa, allowing yourself to be indulged because you choose to. Take yourself on a hike and observe the flow of breath and the sound of the Earth around you. Remember who YOU are so that you do not get lost in the label of being someone else's partner. Take yourself on a date.

Rule # 2: Have a silent date night with your partner. Pick a night that you will both spend together at home, but choose to spend the evening in a mutual silence of observation. Do what you do and allow your partner the same. There is more than one way to listen to your partner, sometimes words spoken can be misinterpreted. Can't handle a whole evening of silence? Try one sit-down dinner in a restaurant and only speak to the servers. Silent observation is not a silent treatment. Listen to your partner's breath, feel their movements, indulge your other senses in "seeing" your partner in different ways.

Rule #3: Zip It! Let's face it, sometimes we just can't shut up! We think we have all the answers to solve our partner's issues. Sometimes we just need to keep our mouths closed and let them figure it out for themselves. No one likes a know-it-all.

Rule #4: Never go to bed angry. Go to bed with a mutual understanding that you have a disagreement. Your differences make you stronger as a unit.

Rule #5: Thank you, Thank you, Thank you. Uh huh, an attitude of gratitude. Being grateful for what you are experiencing in life in this moment has profound effects. Instead of thinking of all the things you wish your partner was or wasn't, feel all of the wonderful things your partner is! Make a gratitude list on your partner if it helps. (Why are you with them?)

Rule #6: The truth may hurt, but at least it's honest. And it feels SOOOOO good. Freedom baby, yeah! Speak the truth with compassion and non-harming as your guide.

Rule #7: Do it, just because you want to do it, not because you're looking for something in return. (Uh huh, you just interpret that in whichever way you need to.)

Rule #8: Life is a choice, as are our relationships. That's right, you choose to do this. Isn't it grand?

Rule #9: Patience, please. I know I don't have all the answers, yet, so please be patient while they come. I promise I will do the same for you. And if you see me being impatient, please come stand by me and take the biggest, most compassionately embracing breath in than you know how to.

Rule #10: Create a safety word. Safety words are a mutually agreed upon term that can be used in the heat of an argument that says to the folk involved, "It's time to take a break." "Maple Tree." See, if someone realizes that it's going too far, speak the word, and agree to take at least a half-hour break (hopefully in separate spaces). In that time, work on YOU, not what your partner/friend/peer/boss, whoever should be doing. This is your time to get your own sense of self back.

Yes, no matter what, it's all gonna be alright. Life is in constant change.

Who do you want to be, today? What is keeping you from being that person?

22. DO YOU MIND?

Help. I'm lost and I don't know where to find me.

Have you ever found yourself completely lost in your own environment. Asking yourself questions like, "Who am I?" Or "How did I get here?"

We've become the employee, the boss, the kid, the parent, the lover, the partner, the husband and wife. We've become everything everyone expects us to be, but we have forgotten to BE ourself.

When we are born, we are not handed a book on how to be a human. We are raised by other people and society. We spend the younger part of our days being the son and daughter, and the student. When we begin to work, we become the employee and possibly the boss. When we enter a relationship we become the partner, lover, husband or wife and possibly a parent. We are always caught in this identity of label and this label creates an expectation of "what should be" based on "what was".

Then one day, maybe in our mid 30's or 40's we have the identity crisis. How did I get here? Who am I? We may notice that we become frustrated more frequently with the people around us and that we get tired of what is being asked of us. Maybe we've resorted to "checking out" either emotionally, psychologically or physically. We may have even started using mind altering substances to help us check out. Wherever you are, you can always find your way back to the YOU that is your truth.

One of the easiest ways to reconnect with yourself is to find the world that exists within you that doesn't pertain to thought. What? A world without thoughts? Sounds impossible, but it does exist. We live in a world of sensation - we are sensational beings, truly. Our mind understands our existence through this interpretation of sensation as we experience in this outside world. The sense of sight shows us where we are in terms of light and dark, sound tells us what is moving around us, taste tells us whether what we are eating is good for us or not, smell helps us determine what is safe and touch allows us to connect on a whole different level.

All of these sensations exist without thought. You do not need to think about the smell of a cup of coffee, it is just there and you experience the smell. Thought comes in and places a value on the sensation - "I like this," or "I do not like that." This thought process takes us away from the experience of what is, to the experience of something other than. This "other than" is the thing that starts to check us out. When we do not want to experience something that is happening, we begin to check ourselves out of it. Even when we do want to experience something, like a romantic touch of a partner, we begin to check out of the experience and go into fantasy mode of imagined thought. Sound complicated?? Look at it this way - we are either aware and involved in what IS as it is happening, or we're off in thought world creating a story.

If we spend 98% of our life off in thought, then we're missing a really big part of our life. Your mind of course will tell you that you cannot exist without your thoughts. It wants your story to continue. It is the ego that creates the story, and it does a VERY good job at it.

To get out of the thought process, you have to practice being in the present moment. You've heard it from a million sources. Life exists here, in the now. In the present moment, there isn't any pain or suffering because there is no story related to a sensation being experienced. There is only sensation. It is the attachment to this sensation that creates suffering. Being in the present moment can happen through awareness of the senses. Practice being with the senses one at a time.

The sense of sight is an easy way to get in touch with the present moment. I find that looking at something nature has created is a beautiful way to get in touch. All you really need is one leaf or flower. Find a place for your item of gazing and sit and begin to look at it. The longer you look at it and the more you pay your attention to just the observation of it, the more the object will show its details to you. Notice the variances of color, shape, texture and saturation.

The sense of sound can be a way to connect as well, depending on what sounds you have in your environment. We are the noisiest creatures on the planet. We have created so much noise, we don't even notice how loud we are anymore. Again, I find that a natural environment (on a mountain hike) is a beautiful way to reconnect to the present because you can listen to the natural sounds of life around you. Notice the constant change of sound. No one moment is the same as another.

Touch is an amazing connector. Whether you are walking down the beach and the hot sand is under your feet, or wading through the water, you can feel through your skin different sensations. Go for a walking meditation. It is simple. Begin to walk very slowly and observe all of the different sensations that are created by movement. Feel the earth pressed up against your feet. Feel the muscles changing and reacting to keep your balance and your momentum moving forward.

While you practice your sensation observations, remember that the mind will want to create a story around them. It is the practice to be aware of that pattern of the mind and return the focus and attention to the task of observation without reaction, which is important.

You can always spend a week in silence. Silence is an amazing way to connect to that existence within you that is always present. Silence from within gets you out of the thinking mind, out of the constant pull to be someone for someone or something other than what is. Silence is an observation. Silence is a practice that doesn't create more noise. Noise is a wonderful mind distractor and thought creator.

The more you practice getting in touch with the present moment, the more you discover who you truly are. You will find that as you practice this, your interactions with others will change; this is okay. You are becoming the existence of YOU. There is no truer benefit to those who know you than finding the person that is you. This is your life, your creation and your journey. Only you can live it.

So the next time you feel that you're lost or have lost touch with your own self, begin the practice of observation, and rediscover the person you truly are. Find the beauty that exists within you, and you will discover a world of beauty around you.

"Don't seek the truth, just cease to cherish opinions." E. Tolle

"I am responsible for my own happiness"

23. OH MY PERNICIOUS MIND

The mind is a terrible thing, and let's face the facts, it wastes no time in letting us know how absolutely wicked it can really be. When we learn how the functions of the mind operate, and why, we can then do something about this appalling brutality it imposes on our perpetual quest for happiness. Once you become aware of your quest, the mind will find every distraction available, throwing obstacle after obstacle in your path to keep you from finding peace. This is what it does. Armed with this information, we can do something about it.

There are four basic parts of mind which all have different functions. They are the Conscious, Sub-Conscious, Ego and Over-mind. Knowing which part of the mind you are seeing life through can help you to understand life itself. When you are unaware, you become lost in the battle between reality and whatever the mind wants you to see.

The Conscious part of the mind interprets the external experience through the senses of the body. It interprets taste, touch, smell, sight and sound, relaying the information to other parts of the brain to categorize and understand. The Conscious part of the mind is connected to the present moment and is constantly deciphering what is manifesting in each moment as it occurs through the sensations of our body. Awareness exists in the conscious mind. This is called consciousness.

The Conscious mind receives information "out there" through the body, so that the Spirit/You "in here" can understand where it is in time and place on this very human voyage of life. The Conscious mind simply understands the external flux and vibration causes waves which come in contact with the body that then get interpreted by this very part of the mind.

The Conscious mind hears music, voices, sounds. It interprets sensations of smell and touch. It is the sensory perception of our existence. The conscious mind can interpret the feel of the air as cold/warm or notice that water is wet. It notices the smell of the Earth after the rain. It recognizes through hearing the sound of a bird chirping. It discovers the taste of a fresh bite of a lemon. It makes sense of seeing the body's relationship in terms of depth and placement. This activity is all Conscious mind level activity. Simply understanding through cognition where the body is at a certain period of time in its own present moment.

The Conscious part of the mind also interprets, analyzes and problem solves. It lets us figure out how to get from point A to point B without even having to see point B. For example, if you are in Seattle and you want to drive to Boston, you do not need to see Boston from Seattle to get there. You need to know that you have to get on a road that heads East.

Once a sensation is experienced, the mind can go one of two ways, Ego or Overmind. When you go to Ego mind, it's going into a story creation of the sensation occurring. "I don't like it, I don't want any more of it, I want it to stop." Emotion is related to the experience. Truthfully it is just sensation. It is occurring. There is no story, we (our ego) create the story. The ego also creates a sense of separation. Housed in the ego is our personality, which is this filter that we see life through. Some of us see through anger, some through fear, some through victim consciousness.

Awareness is the thing that tells you you're awake and experiencing the present moment unfolding. Awareness sits in the **Over-mind**. This part of the mind is choicelessly aware of the fact that sensations are occurring in this external world experience, or in the experiences being received by the body, but does not place a value or judgment on the experiences themselves. It notices there is sensation occurring constantly and is in constant change, but does not have attachment or aversion to the particular sensations, because in truth, sensations (like all things), are constantly changing form. No one moment is, or has ever been, the same. It notices, through the sense of sight, that someone has walked into the room, but does not create a story of lust or revulsion depending on who it was that has just entered. That is the job of the Ego mind.

The Over-mind is a focused mind that can hold two or more points of view simultaneously. It understands that there is pressure, vibration, heat, coolness, dryness, moisture and so on, but it does not create story and react. It is the intuitive part of the mind where intellect is transformed into higher intuition.

The Ego places value or judgement on that which you are experiencing externally. It has a job. It is territorial and defensive. It tells us stories about the sensations that we experience. It decides between "I like this" and "I don't like that." It takes a simple sensation and creates a novel around it. The Ego also identifies itself with these sensations and stories. Label, story, agenda: these are all part of the ego mind. In reality, the only thing that exists is the present moment, in each moment. The ego mind flits from past to future and back again a gazillion times (gazillion is one of those not-so-scientifically astronomical numbers somewhere in the "lots of extra zero's" range) It, the Ego, is on a never ending, misguided search for finding happiness "out there".

Another thing about the ego mind is its insatiable appetite for chaos. It wants our attention to be focused on anything but the present moment, because the Ego does not exist in the present moment. When you are in the here and now, the Ego is nowhere to be found. It can't be: there is no space for consciousness (awareness of present) and Ego in the same existence. But here's the thing - the Ego is REALLY good at it's job. You can just ask yourself to find out the truth: Do I spend my time thinking about past or future, or am I witness to each moment as it comes to pass?

How often do you find yourself beaten up by your own thoughts and stories? Some "thing" happens in this external world, and we go off in creation mode thinking things about the "what was," and the "next time I'll do this" scenarios. Typically these thoughts are not pleasant, though even the pleasant thoughts do not serve us well. Either way, pleasant or unpleasant, thoughts create a story to take us away. Then we react to this (unless of course we're aware of the thoughts). Our reactions can either be physical, mental and/or emotional, which all play into each other.

Let's say you experience a sensation on the body. Your conscious mind interprets the sensation so that it can be identified, the Sub-conscious mind stores the sensory input, and the Ego instantly starts to create a story (unless of course, it's already hell-bent on another story of its own creation). When you are aware of the sensations that are manifesting in each moment, you can then CHOOSE to take action. When you are unaware, you move into the re-action mode of the ego mind. This is where the ego takes over to create story. Sometimes the stories are "fun" and interesting, other times they're just plain 'ole mean. Thought then feeds the emotion, which feeds the sensation, which then feeds the thought, which feeds the emotion...and so the story goes.

You've heard the expression that people think themselves sick. This is how it happens. Unfortunately for most of us, we are completely unaware of the fact that we're doing it to ourselves. Then, the Ego is clever enough to blame something "out there" for what we're experiencing "in here." So nice of it, isn't it? Yes, I'll have another scoop of Ego mind please, with chocolate sprinkles.

The **Ego** mind is our very chattery, judgmental, story holding and creating monkey mind. It is the thing that flits from the past to the future, continually pulling us away from the experiences of the present moment to feed it's need for survival by creating stories about the sensations that are being experienced. It judges what is being experienced in the body presently, compares those experiences to things it remembers in the past, and then starts to
"like" (attachment) or "dislike" (aversion) the sensations.

One of the ways I've come to understanding my mind is it is likeness to a hurricane. When we are in the chattery ego mind, flitting from story to story, the "should, could and would have's of life" to the "next time I'm going to," it is like being tossed around in the winds. There is no way of knowing which way is up, down or otherwise. We are just being forced around a whirling dervish of chaos. However, when we focus the mind, when we train it to be present to the experiences of life unfolding, here and now, we become the center of this chaotic storm. We become the eye of our own mind hurricane and it is a calm, peaceful place to be. We become pure awareness. Present. This is the place the Ego strives to take us away from, and again, IT is very good at its job. (Alpha Poem for **EGO** - **E**veryone's **G**ot **O**ne)

The **Subconscious** mind is a storehouse of all the external experiences that have occurred and been witnessed by your body. It is like your hard-drive of your computer system. If you have an overactive, chatterbox mindset, it is highly unlikely that you will have direct access to this warehouse of conscious impressions. However, if you can train your mind to be still and focused, you will find that the gates to this part of the mind become open to you.

If you're looking to make change with your chatterbox mind, you have to overhaul your subconscious mind. You have to wipe the slate clean, and tear apart your belief systems. Be free of what you think things *should* be so that you can experience what they *are*. You have to let go of the concepts of what you believe something to be. If you can only see it one way, you're missing out on the opportunity to see it in many other ways. You're stuck. You start living in one pointed view. But changing this, by being aware, allows you to see things in multiple points of view in many perspectives. You get to see a full perspective of life, and you get to see that life mirrored back as your creative world experience.

Can you be a part of a complete moment without passing judgment on any part of it?

Once you start to do the work to get out of this ego world of existence, you start to move into the over-mind. This is your intuitive part of the mind. The place where you know something to be the truth regardless of any story associated with it. It's where intellect is transformed into higher intuition. It sees differences and variances of sensations, but does not place value or judgment on what it experiences. When you're in over-mind, you are choicelessly aware without creating judgments. You are in awareness, so you are in present moment. When you are in thought, you are in ego. When you are in over-mind, you can hold multiple points of view on the same object at the same time and from this perspective, there is no judgment.

The ego defends, protects and is territorial. Who are you? When that question is asked, you have this entire story of your past that tells you who you are. This is the Ego's story - attachment to identity of something that was. The truth is that YOU are constantly unfolding from moment to moment. This mindset of "who we are" is false - it is who we were, or perhaps, what we've experienced. When someone tells you you're "not" this story - the ego gets angry and defends it.

What part of the mind are you in in THIS moment? What part of the mind is interpreting the situation? If there is conflict, ask what part of the mind you are in. Are you just observing? Are you in conscious mind? Are you placing a value or judging the experience? Are you allowing yourself to see other possibilities or points of view?

This internal world experiences this external world because we feel it, see it, smell it, and hear it. Conscious part of mind recognizes these sensations to give you a perspective of your existence in time and place. The over-mind is aware of the fact that it is happening. Conscious interprets, and the over-mind is choicelessly aware. The opposite would be ego - creating a story, placing a value or judgement on the sensation that is occurring, taking you away from the sensation itself and disappearing into thought. Subconscious is the storehouse of all conscious impressions.

The ego is really good at what it does. (Has this been mentioned before?) It says it is your leader and has you so convinced that it is you. It says you cannot exist without it. It is a liar. It is not the truth. It is not your existence. You can be free of it.

Have you ever recognized an in-depth experience you've had with the present moment? Perhaps it was vibrant, calm, or even surreal. Maybe you realized you were there, maybe you didn't. Part of the yoga practice is to go to this place, practice going there, over and over again. The more you practice going there, the more you can get there easily. That is why it is a yoga *practice*. Some people wake up and they're there, and they're there for life. Sometimes the bigger gifts come from doing the work to get there. But in truth there is no THERE to get to. You are already here.

Have you ever had to give someone directions on how to get from here to there, when they have not travelled the road, but you have? If you've travelled the road only once, your directions may be short and inconclusive at times, but you have a general idea of where to point them. If this road is something that you travel on a regular basis, then you will know it in detail, and explaining it to a foreigner would not be a problem. The same principle applies to becoming present to your own presence. The more you teach yourself to be present, the easier it is to be in the experience. You have travelled down the road, you recognize it, and so you have a guidance system internally from experience that can help to bring you back to it over and over again. Practice!

What can we do? Of course I'm going to say Yoga, as the very essence of yoga is clarity of mind. Yoga is a training of the mind. In that, there are other things you can do to train the mind, like martial arts, tai chi, sports, and a whole lot more. What it comes down to is wanting to train the mind to be non-reactive, to be at perfect ease no matter what position the body is in, or what sensations it is experiencing (after all, this too shall pass). The body position, really, is just a place to be. It is the mind's reaction to the story created about the position of the body that gets us into trouble.

It is easy to blame the world around you for your misery, but as you **are** the world around you, you're really only blaming yourself. Make an attempt to see the stories your mind creates about the experiences in your surroundings. And also make an attempt to not hold those stories as your identity. You are not them, and they are not you. You are an ever-evolving creation, constantly changing from moment to moment, full of life, love and compassion. You are the only person responsible for your happiness.

"I see the beauty in all that surrounds me. I am part of this creation and also the creator. I am not separate but part of the whole." (Breathing helps!)

24. THE KLESHAS

Yoga Sutra II-6 - *Egoism is the enmeshing function of the mind as an instrument of perception as if it were the seer's power of consciousness.*

"I" perceive "this" from *my* point-of-view, putting *myself* into YOUR seat, the rightful seat of life, without you even knowing. You've been dethroned and you have no clue. You are this wonderfully beautiful creator, but you've been knocked aside so that "I" can have my way with you. Who am "I"?

Kleshas are 5 root obstructions - Roots causes of suffering from the mind.

Avidya - Ignorance - The leader of the remaining obstructions, is not knowing. It simply means being unaware. When you are unaware that something is happening, you cannot do anything about it. Once you become aware, you can make conscious change. Trying to make change "out there" is difficult. But when you make change from the inside (your perception), the outside begins to match.

We're constantly trying to make things happy out here, so we feel happy on the inside... but it's the complete opposite of that if you want it to work. If you want to be happy, find places inside that make you feel happy and cultivate that, so it spreads through your existence and overflows and everyone out there gets to experience that. You'll create so much of it in you, other people start to feel happy about themselves too.

Ignorance is not seeing the nature of our oneness - internal/external. It sees life as separate. I believe life is a mirror reflecting back everything from the inside. If you want to see the beauty out there, you have to find it inside first. Unawareness (ignorance) creates separation between people, making boarders, and boundaries. We put up fences because we think that others are taking away from us. We call them others because we see them as separate from us. We do not see them as ourselves.

Unawareness is the root of all the others. First you must become aware, then you can make change.

Asmita - "I Am" - the story from the ego perspective. Our Ego identifies with our body, as opposed to the body being the vehicle between your internal and external. This also creates separation. The body is not you, it is something that is carrying you. It is your house and your vehicle. When that vehicle is clean and healthy, your perceptions are clean and healthy. You're not fat, your body may be over-fat. You are pure existence, energy flow, experiencing a world of external through a body that is carrying excess. In ego we have need for defense/protection which leads to pride, envy, and competition. After all, if we have a story, it must be true and it must be defended!

Raga - Attachment - "Like". When we are attached to something, a thought, we're projecting into the future an expectation for a desired result. So what happens? I'm not going to be happy until I have ____. (Fill in the blank.) Expectation leads to disappointment - we get what we want and we want more. We don't get what we want and we create a story about it by becoming the victim of the circumstance. We get attached to people, and when they don't act as we think they should act we become angry and resentful. (Think "Fatal Attraction") We get angry at others when our expectations aren't met. Isn't that interesting? "Because you're not living your life the way I see you have potential to live it, I get angry with you." We're so kind and caring, aren't we? Just wanting what's "best" for those who we love. Mmm hmmm. We live in a state of comparison that leads to envy, disappointment and delusion. Because, after all, if I only have what YOU have, I'll be happy. Just don't try to take what I have away.

Dwesha - Aversion - "Dislike" or dividing ourselves from others. Separating yourself from others, because, let's face it, they're just not as good as you are. "My God, my religion, my country, my marriage are better than yours. In fact, your God is just a figment of your imagination, because obviously only my God can be the *right* one." Dislike creates hatred and puts us into psychological sleep - checking out of reality, the present, to escape to something more fantasy oriented in the mind. This leads to depression, repression of emotions, self-hatred, self-blame. Then we take that self-blame and self-hatred and project it onto anyone who we feel is unworthy. We then label them and create hate campaigns against them. Shall we list some examples? What kind of emotions do you feel when you hear these words: Illegals, Niggers, Fags, Whores, Jews, Towel Heads, Nazis. Do you feel anger? Pity? Sadness? Righteous? Do you dis-like yourself for thinking these things? Are you blaming someone else for how you feel about what you've just read? Look to see where you are falling into societal labels of others because society has deemed them "less than" you. Or, perhaps society is trying to label you down into one small insignificant and inappropriate label that you are far to beautiful to fit into.

Abinivesa - "Fear." What is fear? What IS fear? What is it that we are afraid of? We can ask this question of anything that creates a sense of anxiety within us. Fear, as it turns out, is a future-based thought obsession based on a past experience. The experience itself could also be in the form of thought, but most likely it is from something we've learned. What are we really afraid of? Heights? Spiders? Small spaces? Layoffs? Clowns?

Perhaps fear of anything is fear of death. If you're afraid of heights, you're afraid of falling to your death. If you're afraid of spiders, you're afraid of getting bit and dying. Claustrophobia is fear of suffocating to death. It is engrained in our existence - fear of death, fear of the unknown. We CLING to life so much out of fear that we forget to live.

What if?? What IF, perhaps, we are afraid to live?

Denny Richard

Is it fear of change?? Really, everything is all change, moment to moment. There is no SAME anything, ever. It is always different. There is nothing more constant than change. Helplessness, guilt, mistrust, and victim consciousness are all related to fear. Aggression and violence are the result of fear. Did someone once tell you to be afraid of death? Did you believe them? Do you still believe them? Did they give you an alternative to life when they told you to be afraid of death? And you still believe them? Why?

We do it to ourselves, this thing called suffering (dukkha). Which is great, because if we realize this we can do something about it. We get to change, with awareness, and we can be aware of the fact that we are changing.

When you come into a conflict, ask yourself if you can be aware that there is conflict without the story being attached to it. There is a story about this conflict that I'm participating in, so there is conflict. Can you be aware of the fact that YOU are in conflict? Can you recognize what it is that is creating the conflict? Are you blaming it on someone? Are you afraid something is going to happen? Are you afraid something is not going to happen? Are you having sensations in the body that you just don't like and you're associating them with everything you're surrounded by? What is causing the triggers? What is causing those trails of thought that pull you away from here into conflict.

*Just when the
caterpillar
thought the
world was over,
it became
a butterfly.*

-Unknown

25. THE VEIL OF "MISS PERCEPTION"

Our mind is like a battlefield, and the outer world of experiences are the weapons the mind uses to create the internal struggle of understanding truth through the senses of our body. The distortion of this truth, through our veil of perception, is what creates the chaos of the mind, or the internal battlefield of attempted understanding. The Baghavad Gita is a story about the mind in its understanding of the chaotic world around you. What it teaches us is that the mind indulges in the external sensations (touch, taste, sight, sound and smell) and through this veil of interpretation creates a pattern of "like" or "unlike" - not too dissimilar to a certain social networking button.

Some of us see through a veil of *anger*, some of us through *fear* and others through the veil of *victim*. We don't often see what is there in truth, but we interpret what we see through our veil. If we have a preconception of a person or event, and that person or event acts in a way similar to what we think, then we tend to hold that story true. The truth of the matter is that every moment is unique and individual to anything that may have happened prior. This belief system we have not only affects us, but the person that we hold the "truth" towards.

This is the gross mind's creation of story about an external experience. The actual truth is that something in the external has happened, which creates a sensation on the body (touch, taste, sight, sound and smell), and before we recognize anything else the mind says, "I like" or "I don't like," and from that point on we drift to a mind story creation of attachment or aversion. "When a man dwells in his mind on the object of sense, attachment to them is produced. From attachment springs desire and from desire comes anger." (Gita 2.62) This is what we experience when we are not getting what we expected to get and blaming another for it.

The difficulty in overcoming this anger, fear or victimhood that dwells as our "existence" is being aware that we are seeing "life out there" through this veil to begin with. My veil is an anger perspective. If something happens in my external world that "I don't like," I react in anger. It is unfortunate for others, and also for me, when this happens because the event itself is not recognized and the truth is veiled by this impostor of "anger". So instead of the message coming through, the message is missed and the person receiving is left with a bunch of anger to sort through. When we can become aware of the fact that we are reacting (like or dislike) we can then breathe and understand that our veil is up and begin to act with awareness. This allows the true message to come across, without being wrapped up in a bunch of garbage that no one wants to experience.

Imagine knowing this information and having a confrontation with a friend. One could perhaps say, "Oh, he/she is reacting to external because of their attachment or aversion to sensations their body is experiencing and I'm receiving this reaction back through their veil". Sounds easy, right? The tough part is being aware this is happening, because we instantly begin to react as well. Tougher still is not only are your friends doing this, but we are too. So we have two veils working against our otherwise effortless communication process.

"What one perceives is a result of inter-plays between past experiences, including one's culture, and the interpretation of the perceived." (Wiki: Perception) The mind is quick, and very often too quick in reacting. We often hold someone else's reaction as the end-all of our interaction with them, dismissing them as evil, hateful, rude, arrogant, hurtful or any other derogatory thought/feeling/emotion we can quickly create about a situation we've had with them. Forgiveness and compassion for others are quickly squelched for their dualistic opposites.

Why do we do this? Perhaps our reactions in those others that create these feelings in us aren't really creating something new, but are highlighting something that already exists within us. All of this energy is always a part of us, but because of our filters, we only experience a small portion of it at certain times. Then someone comes along and does something and we begin to react because that energy that is in us starts to stir. Those people are our button pushers. The emotions that have been building and bubbling on our back burners for ages quickly percolate to the top because of "that" person/event.

Breathe. Know that it will all be okay. Know that even though you might have moments that don't feel great, these moments too will pass. Forgive other's who have "wronged" you, yes, but first you must forgive yourself for holding onto the story about this person. In truth, if you're hurt, it's *your* hurt, and the thing that continually punishes you is your own "Veil of Miss-Perception" story. The event is over and done - what's done is done, and cannot be undone. What can change is our attachment to the story which continually punishes us and makes us miss out on friendships, love, and family. You are this powerful. You are this important. You can do this.

"I forgive you, and I hope you can find it in yourself to also forgive me," says the man to the man in the mirror.

Peace.

26. RECOVERY

We often hear the term recovery in the "Anonymous" groups. These groups claim that we are in a constant state of recovery. When I first heard this, I had a very negative reaction. "Why are people being taught that they will never get better?", was my question. I interpreted, "constantly being in recovery," as an expression that says you can never be free. Not being free means you are stuck or bound by some flawed existence of the past. This is a miserable state of existence.

If you've ever had an addiction and have come to understand that what you have done was unhealthy and have moved on from it, then you are free from the addictive substance. Truthfully, it is not a "substance" we are addicted to, but the mind's attachment to the sensations that are being experienced in the body due to the substance which has been introduced. The substance could be anything (drugs, alcohol, thoughts, emotions, people, energy, sex, internet, movies, television).

If a musician were to focus his or her attention to the one missed musical note in a phrase, they would never *recover* and the rest of the musical piece they were playing would be nightmarish at best. The musician needs to be able to recover from an error and move FORWARD, reconnecting themselves back to the experience of the expression of the present moment to create and share. If an athlete were to make a bauble on a play and were to think to himself, "Gosh, because I have done this, I must now be in recovery so I do not make the same error again," they would never become accomplished at their sport. After all, a moment to one is an eternity to another.

How long do we hold onto the story of our apparent misstep before we let it go? How long do we let it be a part of our "story." This story is the mind's self-preservation attempt at trying to define "who I am." What it says is, "yes I've gone through this experience, and I wouldn't be who I am without it." That is all fine and dandy to understand, but when we hold onto that story we become addicted in another fashion. We become addicted to the story of our own mind, constantly craving to let it be that thing which defines us. The self-preserved "I am-ness" of our so called life. Are we really so limited?

Am I telling you to throw away your connection to recovery programs? No. That would be silly. They are obviously very helpful to many people. The question I do ask, however, is "when can you let go of the story?"

So, what have I learned? Recovery is a constant process? In one aspect. The viewpoint of the Anonymous groups is that we are perpetually falling off the wagon, so we must be in a constant state of recovery to keep ourselves from hitting the ground. To me, this is a constant state of victimhood. Is this really healing, or does it enable us to stay in that story? What this understanding has taught me, is that we are constantly recovering from "life." Or perhaps, we are recovering from the experiences of life that attempt to force us into a creation of story in the mind. These are the very things that prevent us from living fully. If we are so attached to our stories, we are constantly allowing the mind to fluctuate from this and that, and in this experience we live no "life" at all.

In truth, I don't know anything other than this moment. All the rest is imagination, a thought process, past or future, memory or anticipation. When we can be present to understand and experience this present moment unfolding, there is choice, conscious choice. Everything is exactly as it is, and that is changing every moment. There are a multitude of "actions" to take at any one given moment in time (so says the mind), but you can only take one action. When you are aware, present, the RIGHT ONE is obvious. That is the one you do. It is always the right one, otherwise you would be doing something else.

When we are doing things that are unhealthy, things that are creating disharmony with the body and mind, we are disconnected to the experience of the present moment. We are unconscious for the most part. Our bodies may be moving, yes, but we are so caught up in the thought of mind we do not recognize our presence. When we do things that are healthy for our growth, you do not have to ask your mind for permission to enjoy it. We often set ourselves up for a miserable experience, because *we think* we need to have permission from our story to experience the greatness of life. It is okay to feel good, but we feel guilty about feeling good because we look around and see that almost everyone around us is miserable. We're told, by others and our mind, that if we're feeling good, we must be doing something bad. That is a lie. If others want to be miserable, let them. It is not your job to fix that. You can, however, recover from your own sense of insanity and begin to feel better now.

"This too shall pass"

27. THE FOG

Walking through a fog
unsure of my surroundings.
My footsteps muffled by
the clouds in which I am shrouded.
I can't see where I'm going.
I couldn't tell you a direction.
But, I know I must keep stepping.
One day, the fog will clear.
One day, I will understand where I am,
and I will be unmistakeable.

(2011)

28. A WALK INTO SILENCE

When it comes to making noise, we humans are the beasts to call upon. We know how to be loud and proud. The mind loves noise. In its endless quest to follow distraction, noise is a trigger for our ego thought. We live in a society here in the USA where we are taught that bigger is better. All around us are bigger TV's, bigger speakers, bigger engines, bigger vehicles (bigger enemies, bigger problems). Even the small things in our existence are noise makers. Clicking pens and watches, espresso machines, white-noise makers, music players, cell phone rings, computers and so much more. We're in a pleasure over-load of noise for the already over-active ego mind.

In our journey along this human life, it is important for us to remember to get back to the basics now and then. We spend so much time creating sensory distractions for our mind, which really just makes it more chaotic when we try to slow it down. Distractions not only come from sound noise, but visual, smell, touch and taste as well. The objects themselves are not the distractions, but the mind's attachment to creating story around the things we are sensing is. The sound of a dog barking is just a sound, but the thought of "I wish the dog would stop barking" is the distraction.

The opposite of noise is silence. The very word sends the ego into a near panic. It does not want to be silenced. If it isn't allowed to wander around from distraction to distraction, it gets restless and attempts to make us restless as well. We have to remember that we are the master, and the ego is not. It only takes a little bit of practice to thwart the efforts of the ego, but it is the practice that matters.

In attempting to walk into silence, there are many avenues you can pursue. Silence in our regular environments is almost impossible to achieve, unless you are one of those goal-oriented folk. The, "I'm going to do this, and nothing is going to get in my way" attitude is what will work if you attempt to find silence at home. This could be as simple as having a day where you do not turn on the radio, television, iPod, and other noise creating devices and allow yourself to observe the sounds that are already in creation. Observation is the key. When we observe the endless cycle of the present moment unfolding, then the ego is at rest and calm. When we are unaware that we've been distracted by thought (attachment, story, aversion, fear) then we are trapped by the ego.

Another way to get into silence is to have a day of personal silence. This is where you are not in communication with another. You can also do this at home. Spend a day where you do not have conversation with another. Turn off the phone and computer and let your friends, family know that you will be honoring a day of silence. This may seem "easy" but there is a need for the mind to follow distraction. Again, it's about not feeding the mind things that would create more distraction. So spending a day without communication but watching a full day of Harry Potter movies is not the practice of silence.

Why would I ever want to go into silence? What is the purpose? When silence is broken, a sound occurs and the conscious part of the mind observes the sound. Then the ego places a value and begins to create a story by creating thought. For example, it would say, "I don't like the jackhammer this early in the morning, I'm not going to get enough sleep, this is a horrible way to start my day," or it may even say, "ooh sounds of lovemaking coming from the apartment next door. I need to pay attention." The value being placed can be of pleasure or pain, attachment or aversion. It can also be out of fear. Hearing a sound in the back-yard late at night might send us along into a panic if we do not keep ourselves under control. Or, we become consciously aware of the change.

When we practice silence, both within and outside of our selves, we practice stilling the over-active mind. The ego mind is a whirl-wind of chaotic thought. It feeds on emotion and value of sensation. The stresses that are caused by the thought process are intense and are quite harmful to living a healthy existence. Stress can be a killer. Stress is our ego mind's fight against the unfolding present moment. It is the never-ending battle of that part of the mind to move against what is currently happening. The dictionary partly defines stress as 'pressure or tension exerted on a material object,' but we can also take the term "material object" and put in the term "present moment." Think of the ego mind as a crowbar torquing our mind out of our awareness of body that we experience through our senses, into its own ego story and thought pattern. If we get pulled away enough, then we feel the physical stress of the body/mind connection (or if we are in ego - it is disconnection).

The practice of finding silence is one way to help us bring that connection of mind and body back together again, where it exists stress free. We have to remember that it takes practice, patience and also persistence to stay present to the moment. The ego will tell us that we will not exist and cannot survive without it, but it is a liar and it is also used to getting what it wants. Truthfully, we can be free of the constant torquing of the ego mind and live in a very calm and present existence with each moment. In that calm existence of awareness, inspiration creates action, more is accomplished because the "monkey-mind" does not get in the way and we feel physically and emotionally free.

Some other inspirational things that may help you to find silence are:
Movie: Into Great Silence, directed by Philip Groning;
Retreat: 10 Day Silent Meditation - www.dhamma.org;
Book: <u>Inviting Silence</u> by Gunilla Norris.

Spend 1 hour in silence and solitude over the next week.

29. JOURNAL ENTRIES

(The following are journal entries that I have written over periods of time.)

on Love

Ahhhh, Love. Isn't it Grand? Then why does it hurt so much?

Truthfully, Love, doesn't hurt at all. Love is a wonderful, caring, warm-hearted expression of spirit that does not expect anything back from giving it out. This is where we get confused.

"I gave you all my love and all you gave me is heartache." So, we put the two together in our mind and say that love hurts. This is completely untrue. Love, is Love. Simply.

The moment we attach an expectation to something we're giving, is the moment we're bound to this expression of hurtful, dissatisfaction and suffering love. Giving, with the expectation of receiving, is NOT love, it is torture.

If you get what it was you were expecting, you are momentarily happy and then the search and expectation for MORE begins again. A constant and endless search for external happiness, never satisfied with what is.

Then, if you don't get what it was you were expecting, it's complete agony, disbelief and disappointment in the person who did not deliver. Shame on them. How could they not have given you love in return for yours? You won't make that mistake again, right?

From this, we start holding back and blocking our love because we do not want to get hurt and we blame others because we're missing out on love. Yet who is doing the blocking and holding back of Love? We are!

Love, simply, because you can.

on Sleep

When you're not living through awareness of the sensations and breath of your body (your yoke), you're not living life. You're trapped in the Ego mind bouncing back and forth between the past and future, reliving in anger, resentment, guilt, shame, or fantasizing about some once-upon-a-time steamy love affair, (or remembering someone else's - saucy). Or you're in the future, planning worrying, fearing, anxious, nervous or again fantasizing about what has not yet come to pass.

This is no Life. This is life asleep. Psychologically asleep. Unawake to the present moment. This is the difference between you and those "enlightened" ones. You're asleep, even while you're "awake." Awake means being present to life unfolding, and experiencing that moment as it is.

The opposite of this is where we are for most of our journey here on Earth. Completely disconnected, lost in thought, checked out through things like mindless television and internet. These are all forms of psychological (mental) sleep.

Physical sleep is when the body is at complete rest without interruption or disturbances from the mind. When we go to bed at night and "sleep" evades us, we become restless, and because our mind is agitated and not able to check out into psychological sleep, we deny our bodies physical rest and say "we cannot sleep," blaming everything on the external for the distractions the mind is reacting to.

Thankfully, you can give your body all the rest it needs, and if your mind is "awake," you can watch your body rest. The funny thing is, at these very periods, you are living life fully awake, but you are so resistant to it. You are craving to check out, but you do not recognize it, so your mind (ego) creates the misery of a sleepless night. Uncomfortable and trying to create the story of unrest. When the truth is, you can lay perfectly still and observe the body resting, which is what it needs anyway.

Here we are spending most of our time "asleep", psychologically checked out, and the very few times it checks in and becomes awake, we get annoyed because it is taking away from our "rest".

on Like/Dislike

As we know, like attracts like. We find it everywhere we go, which is great. When we find something we like to do, then we find someone who shares that interest and we begin to form bonds with humanity. Great people, growing, creating, expressing and sharing wonderful loving things.

But what about "Don't Like?" "Don't like" tends to lead to fear, anger and hatred. Simply because we do not understand or know any different. When we find that we're *against* something, it's most likely possible that we just don't understand how someone else could possibly like it.

This creates chaos and disharmony within, which we are so willing to share. So, that which was within, quickly comes out and then others eagerly take it into them to make it their own and then begin to share it as well.

If you "don't like it," then don't eat it. Physically, mentally, emotionally, do not take it into your system. Let it be as it is. If you don't like the theater, then don't go to a show. If you don't like open toed shoes, do not wear them. If you don't like gay marriage, then don't marry a gay person.

The trick is to not let your "dislikes" become your hatreds. When you don't like something, and you are paying all of your attention to it, that thing which you do not like becomes stronger in *your* life. That which you resist persists. Where your mind goes, your energy flows. The more energy you put into it (positive or negative) the more shows up in YOUR life. It's not the stronger it gets "out there," but the stronger it gets inside of you, which you then see reflected out there in things around you. You resist it so much that it surrounds you because of your energy (like attracts like), and then you blame IT because you're in the middle of it all. Has this happened to you before?

Ok, so you don't like something, it isn't for you. That is great awareness and a clue for you to move onto something else. If you haven't trained your mind to be present and content with what IS, in this moment, then the tendency will be to focus on the negative aspects of what you do not want. At least try to put your mind to the things you DO want, like and wish to have instead of fantasizing, worrying and hating the things you don't like.

After all, it's *your* hatred for that thing, not anyone else's, that keeps you miserable with it.

on Relationships

Whose life are you living? Hopefully you answered, your own. Otherwise you have got a LOT of work to do. (It's okay, I'll hold your hand).

Would you ever want/expect/be able to live the life someone else is dictating for you to live? Truthfully, no. You'd be miserable if you were. Then how could you possibly expect anyone to live the life you expect THEM to live? Oh, you don't do that? Really? Really?

Have you ever gotten mad at anyone (parent, spouse, lover, child, sibling, best friend) because they didn't do, or act, in a way that you thought would be the best way for them? You know, when your partner doesn't fold the clothes the way you want them folded, do the dishes the way you want them done, love you the way you expect them to? Yet, if they get mad at you for not complying to how it is *they* expect you to live, it is just plain silly, because, after all it's your life to live.

Take a look at your conflicting relationships. See where you are blaming another for the conflict and notice if that conflict is because, "It would be better and easier if *they* just..."

The only life you're responsible for <u>living</u> is your own, not your spouse's, parent's, child's, teacher's, hero's, boyfriend's, girlfriend's, pet's, student's, lover's or preacher's. Does that take a little pressure off, or is it more frightening to know that the only one you're truly responsible for is YOU.

Encourage people to discover their own beautiful journey of life unfolding while you discover yours. But never expect or demand that they live the life you dream for them. That is putting them into binds, and they (and you) will suffer tremendously for it.

on Parenting

The main reason for sex is procreation, which humans could really use a lot less of. We've over-propagated. We're living longer and our Mother can't support us much longer. But I digress...

Why do we have kids? So we can love them unconditionally and support them in discovering everything about themselves and what they want to be for themselves in their life, without expecting anything back in return?

Or, perhaps it's our clinging to our own life, a manner of self-preservation. A mini-me way to keep our life going in another. Expectation that my child will carry my life forward with everything I impart to them. Yeah, good luck with that.

Your right as a parent is given up the moment it was chosen not to pull out. As kids, we expect our parents to fill this role as a loving, nurturing, guiding hero and so often those expectations are not met. Yet again, we blame our parents for that.

Some parents are not meant to be parents. They are accidental parents. They're not better or worse than the parents on purpose, but it is our image of what we expect our parent to be for us that creates our adult disharmony.

It's not very different in reverse. We expect our child to act a certain way that we/society deem appropriate. That doesn't make it right.

Denny Richard

Did you ever notice that the best kid's adventure stories are the ones where the parents are either dead, removed or conveniently unavailable? You don't have to be any of those to let your child live their amazingly adventurous life, but you <u>do</u> have to let <u>them</u> live <u>their</u> life as <u>they</u> choose.

Don't worry, if you love them unconditionally, and support them, they will ask you for your guidance and also make beautiful choices. Otherwise you may find yourself with a rebel (long live the rebels).

30. MY LAST BREATH

The birth of a man is the birth of his sorrow. The longer he lives, the more stupid he becomes, because his anxiety to avoid the unavoidable death becomes more and more acute. What bitterness! He lives for what is always out of reach! His thirst for survival in the future makes him incapable of living in the present.
                                                    Chaung Tzu

We share an undeniable fate, you and I. Just like all that has ever come to be will also pass, you and I will too. There is no denying it. How often do you pay attention to this? Have you even considered what will happen?

Has anyone ever told you to be afraid of death? Has anyone ever given you a conditional expression for life? "Believe in what I tell you, or your after-life will be hell." Have you heard these words? Have you made them your truth? Why? Why would you ever put energy into something that is so negative? Who told you to believe these things? Why do you choose to listen? Who made them the authority on your death? Why have you given them so much power in your life? Do they teach this so they can punish and torture people into giving them what they want? "If you don't believe in what I tell you to believe in, you must be a bad person, my enemy. If you are my enemy then we are at war." Stop!

I refuse to believe in anything so cruel. That belief only feeds their negative thinking machine. The moment someone tells me, "Believe in what I tell you, or else," I kindly smile and walk away. I will not participate. Life is (you are) too amazing to fit into that category of ignorance.

We tend to fear that which we do not know, and our end of life is not something we want to spend time understanding. Why do we avoid it? It is important to understand your last breath. The first thing we do when we are born is breathe in. The last thing we will do as our body dies is breathe out. We spend all of this time preparing for our "future," while completely ignoring that our future is death. Being aware that you are taking your final breath out would be the biggest reward to life. It should feel free and full of love.

We are delicate creatures, whose every breath is connected to this experience called life. This is how important breathe is; without it, we do not exist here. One day, our mind will have to leave our body. One day we will be forced out of our home, our body. Are you ready?

Have you practiced dying? Are you preparing yourself for your final moment? Practicing dying is not morbid. It is a beautiful honor to the life that you are living. Would you want to die in fear and panic when you can die peacefully and fully aware?

Savasana, the pose of the corpse, is a yoga asana (posture) that teaches us how to die consciously. Most of the yoga classes I've ever been to (and taught) end in this pose. We lay there and "relax" into the support of the ground beneath us. But do most of us relax there? I often find my students are very restless in this pose. Unwilling to let the body be, they feel the need to constantly adjust anything to keep themselves from laying in perfect stillness.

This pose has taught me to let go of every mind attachment to my physical body. It has taught me to just be a witness to the sensations that the body is experiencing, without clinging to the body with my mind. I imagine this is what it will be like to die, seeing my mind be free from the home it's been living in.

Meditation is a great teacher of awareness. I cannot stress enough how important it is for you to do your own work. Do not rely on any mythical story to set you free. You must do it yourself; others can only guide you. I believe in you!

Sogyal Rinpoche has written a wonderful book called <u>The Tibetan Book on Living and Dying</u>. In this book, he shows us ways of accepting death as a natural part of life. It is going to happen to all of us one day. Will you be prepared?

Studying death has really taught me is how to live life more fully and compassionately. Because when I see someone I want to initially judge, I remember, "Yes, this person too shall pass." They are in the same realm that I am in, going through their life, with their experience, and most likely wishing they felt better. We are all destined for the same future. Remember to love and to practice being peaceful inside of yourself.

One day, this life too, shall pass.

Where does this leave us? What have we learned? What are we willing to share? Whose lives are we living? In order to grow as a society, we must learn to accept each other and love each other. We must get past these social barriers that create war. We are all humans. We are all on a beautiful journey of life with all of our glorious perspectives. None of them are right, none of them are wrong.

To see the change in the world around you, you must cultivate the change you want to see within you first. It has to start with you. The teachers, saints, gurus, enlightened ones - they are only guides. They can only guide us so that we step onto a path that brings us closer to our own reflection of our true self. That which we see in ourselves, can be easily understood by seeing who and what are reflected back at us. For those that cause pain, let us learn how to heal. For those that create war, let it guide us to peace.

Keep following YOUR path to your higher self. Do not worry what others are doing. Do what you must to become more aware of the beautiful life you are fortunate to live. Mirror/Mirror - it reflects in both directions. Allow yourself to see the beauty in all things. See yourself in all that surrounds you.

Peace ☮

I am immortal every day. I just happen to be traveling in a human body at the moment. This too shall pass.

RESOURCES

Books
Asana Pranayama Mudra Bandha
Swami Satyananda Saraswati ISBN: 8186336141

Hatha Yoga Pradipika
Swami Muktibodhananda ISBN: 8185787387

The Bhagavad Gita
Translated by Eknath Easwaran ISBN:0915132354

Eat, Taste, Heal - an Ayurvedic Guidebook and cookbook for Modern Living, written by Thomas Yarema, MD, Daniel Rhoda, DAS and Chef Johnny Brannigan

The Tibetan Book of Living and Dying
Sogyal Rinpoche ISBN: 0062507931

DVD
Patanjali's Yoga Sutras - Rama Jyoti Vernon - www.internationalyogacollege.org
Yoga Unveiled - www.yogaunveiled.com
Shortcut to Nirvana - www.melafilms.com
Doing time Doing Vipassana - www.dhamma.org/en/av/dtdv.shtml

Teachers and Schools
Rama Jyoti Vernon - www.InternationalYogaCollege.org
Shradda Hartung - www.7Centers.com
Meditation: SN Goenka - www.dhamma.org
Peaceful Roots - www.peacefulroots.com

ABOUT THE AUTHOR

Denny Richard considers everything on his path a teacher of life.

Born and raised in a suburb of Boston, MA. Denny spent many summers traveling the country with Drum and Bugle Corps. There he learned the rewards and benefits of teamwork, dedication and loyalty. At Northeastern University, he studied business management, which prepared him for his job as a financial analyst and gave him the skills to open his own business.

After leaving the corporate world behind, he sought training modalities that would give him the tools he needed to help aide people along their paths to wellness. He is certified by The American College of Sports Medicine (ACSM) as a personal trainer and Hatha Yoga through Fitness Resource Associates (FRA).

In 2006, he moved to Arizona to pursue a 200 hour yoga certification at the Seven Centers in Sedona. This 30 day intensive study changed his life. In 2009, he opened Peaceful Roots, a Therapeutic Yoga and Holistic Fitness center in Phoenix, AZ., allowing him to finally walk his path.

In 2011, he took his passion and skills to Portland, OR. Just as he knows there is more than one avenue to a fully lived life, his life experience has taught him the many ways to achieve harmony and peace. He hopes this book will point you in the direction of your happiness.

"Feeling better all starts with changing your mind. Life is full of amazing adventures, a continual process unfolding to us moment by moment. There are many paths to full liberation and each of us creates his own path. We take the best of everything we have learned from the various places we have touched upon, and walk the path that works for us. No one path is better than another for they all lead us to the same place. When we use yoga and meditation to help us along that path, the path becomes clearer every moment of every day."

Be Happy. Be Peaceful.

www.ingramcontent.com/pod-product-compliance
Lightning Source LLC
Chambersburg PA
CBHW061446040426
42450CB00007B/1235